BONES FROM AWATOVI

NORTHEASTERN ARIZONA

PAPERS OF THE PEABODY MUSEUM OF ARCHAEOLOGY AND ETHNOLOGY

HARVARD UNIVERSITY, VOLUME 70, NUMBERS 1 AND 2

BONES FROM AWATOVI

NORTHEASTERN ARIZONA

Number 1
THE FAUNAL ANALYSIS
Stanley J. Olsen

Number 2
BONE AND ANTLER ARTIFACTS
Richard Page Wheeler

Reports of the Awatovi Expedition
Report No. 11

PEABODY MUSEUM OF ARCHAEOLOGY AND ETHNOLOGY

HARVARD UNIVERSITY • CAMBRIDGE, MASSACHUSETTS

1978

A current list of all publications available can be obtained
by writing to the Publications Department
Peabody Museum, Harvard University
11 Divinity Avenue, Cambridge, Massachusetts 02138

BONES FROM AWATOVI

Number 1
THE FAUNAL ANALYSIS
Stanley J. Olsen

Contents

Figures

Acknowledgments

I wish to thank both Carla A. Martin and Keith M. Anderson of the Arizona Archaeological Center of the United States National Park Service, for their assistance in obtaining funding for this project through NPS Grant CX 8000 50011. Without this support it would not have been possible to undertake the faunal analysis of Awatovi.

I especially want to thank Mrs. Arthur C. Fallon and Dr. Watson Smith, whose generous support made it possible to bring this project to completion.

Dr. J.O. Brew, Director of the Awatovi Expeditions, was instrumental in first making the collections available to me for initial study. Dr. Stephen Williams, former director of the Peabody Museum of Archaeology and Ethnology at Harvard University, granted permission to have the animal bones sent to me at the University of Arizona for analysis and obtained the necessary help to pack, crate, and ship this huge collection of animal bones. My thanks also to Drs. Watson Smith, J.A. Lancaster, and R.P. Wheeler, members of the Harvard Awatovi Expedition, for their patience and help with the many inquiries that were made regarding their original work on the site and for visiting Awatovi with me in May 1975.

Graduate students in the Department of Anthropology at the University of Arizona rendered valuable assistance with the enormous task of identifying the 37,000 fragments of bone that constitute the Awatovi faunal collection. The excellent photographs of the referred specimens are the work of Susan Luebbermann of Tucson.

Figure 1. A, anterior and B, left lateral views of a skull of a modern domestic, scimitar-horned goat of mixed breed similar to those found at Awatovi; C, D, E, and F, horn cores of domestic scimitar-horned goats from Awatovi; G, left lateral and H, frontal aspects of a cranium, with horn core bases, of an Awatovi goat.

Introduction

Up until about a decade ago it was a rare exception when an archaeological project included the collection and preservation of all nonhuman faunal materials from the site under investigation. Notable among these early exceptions was the foresight of Dr. J.O. Brew, Director of the Awatovi, Arizona, Expedition of the Peabody Museum, to save and catalogue by provenience all of the bones encountered by the archaeologists during the years of excavation beginning in 1935 and terminating in 1939.

More typical of the times were the excavations conducted at the contemporary Spanish site of Hawikuh near Zuni, New Mexico, by the Hendricks-Hodge Expedition of 1917-1923. The few animal bones that were saved by the archaeologists were sent by F.W. Hodge to the United States National Museum for identification. Gerrit S. Miller of the Divison of Mammals responded in a letter to Hodge, dated August 31, 1917, in which he stated "We are retaining for the museum most of the bird remains and a few mammals. The rest, according to your instructions, have been destroyed" (Smith, Woodbury, and Woodbury 1966). No analysis of these vertebrates was published. In 1920 Hodge sent another lot of animal bones to the American Museum of Natural History for identification. However, only passing reference is made to a domestic goat, cow, horse, and several dog burials, but no related details of this fauna were published in the Hawikuh report.

During the intervening years between the end of the fieldwork at Awatovi in the 1930s and 1974 this collection was stored in the attic of the Peabody Museum in Cambridge. Dr. Stephen Williams, former director of the Peabody Museum, of course realized the importance of this collection as a means of furnishing information relating to the overall analysis of Awatovi Ruin and was instrumental in making the entire collection available as a basis for the following report.

Nowhere, to my knowledge, has a collection approaching that from Awatovi been amassed which represents the domestic animals that were utilized by colonial Spaniards in the Southwest. The quality of these remains is such that a valid interpretation of the kinds and sizes of various animals was arrived at. In at least one instance the identified species represents the oldest recovered remains of that animal in the New World (domestic cat, *Felis domesticus* from room 505).

The task of determining the associations of the fauna with various units of the ruin was made easier by having access to the report published by the excavators who collected the animal remains (Montgomery, Smith, and Brew 1949). This information was most important in determining whether the animal bones were from rooms or other areas designated for housing livestock by the Franciscans during their occupation of the mission buildings or whether the livestock was kept in rooms that were added to the mission by the Hopis in the period following the Pueblo Revolt of 1680 after abandonment by the Spanish. The beginnings of the Indian village at Awatovi sometime in the early thirteenth century, the founding of Awatovi Mission, its construction, occupation, abandonment, and ultimate destruction are covered in some detail in this previous report and need not be repeated here.

There are no compiled volumes devoted solely to the domestic animals that were utilized by the Spanish in colonial times. Such information occurs as sparse references in various accounts, beginning with the chronicles of the Spanish explorers of the Western Hemisphere. Bits and pieces of additional information can be gleaned from many sources, such as the *Codex Florentino* or from seemingly unrelated publications of more modern articles relating to the history of weaving practices of southwestern Indians, in which mention is made of the various kinds and breeds of sheep and goats either preferred or rejected as sources of wool for weaving. As a further check on suspected races or breeds of animals from Awatovi, the skeletons of identified breeds or races of domestic animals were used for comparison with the animal bones from Awatovi. Some of the more important comparisons have been selected for illustrating in this report (fig. 1).

Important osteological collections have been preserved from other Spanish colonial sites that are in need of faunal comparison with one another as well as with Awatovi. Notable among these are Gran Quivira, New Mexico; Quiburi, Arizona; and Casa de Huesos, Mexico.

If publication of the Awatovi bone material encourages

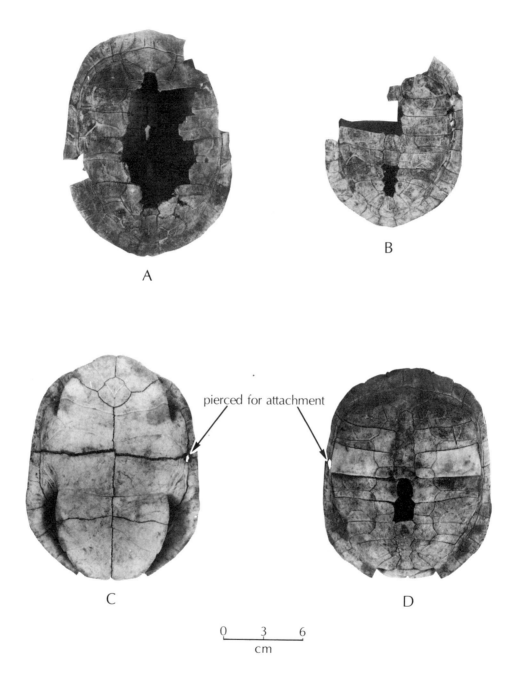

pierced for attachment

Figure 2.   A, B, C, and D, carapace and plastron of painted turtles found in close proximity to the lower limbs of human burial no. 85 from room 434 at Awatovi. The drilled holes for thong attachment indicate their use as dance rattles.

the continuation of such faunal analysis or if it aids the worker who is faced with the identification of domestic animals in the New World, it will have served its purpose.

FISH AND AMPHIBIANS

No fish or amphibian remains were collected at Awatovi. Small size of the elements and nonuse of screens by the excavators could possibly account for their being over-looked if they were present. Although the cartilaginous nature of amphibian bone does not generally lend itself to preservation, examples have turned up in several South-western sites having conditions of preservation similar to those present at Awatovi. The absence of fish may be due in part to a lack of interest in this food source or a possible taboo against fish, or these animals may not have been available in close proximity to the mesas. At any rate they are absent from the faunal collections.

REPTILES

The reptiles of Awatovi are known only from the cara-paces and plastrons of the western painted turtle (*Chrysemys picta belli*). Four complete shells were found with postrebellion human burial no. 85, located in room 434. They were obviously used as leg rattles (fig. 2), inasmuch as the drilled holes for attachment thongs are present in all specimens. The construction or method of attachment to the wearer is the same as that used today by

the Hopis. Several carapace and plastron fragments of this same species of turtle were recovered from rooms 523, 620, and 705. They were not associated with human burials. However, they do not represent the area of the shell where the drilled holes occur and it is not possible to state whether or not they represent fragments of rattles.

The occurrence of this turtle at Awatovi is interesting in that it is not a common resident of the state at the present time. There is a possibility that it may occur in the extreme southeastern portion of Arizona, but more detailed inves-tigation is needed in order to establish if in fact it does. *Chrysemys* does occur in central New Mexico from north to south. The reptile also occurs in southern Utah to the northern limits of Arizona.

The animal occurs to altitudes over 6,000 feet above sea level and prefers quiet shallow waters. It frequents ponds, marshes, small lakes, and gentle streams. Whether this turtle was brought from its range outside the area of Antelope Mesa or whether it ranged nearby in the seven-teenth century is not known.

The carapace is ideally suited for use as a rattle as it is lightly constructed and averages from 4 inches to 9 inches in length (the Awatovi examples are 6¾ inches long). This shell would seem to be more desired by the dancers than would the more common, heavily built desert gopher tortoise (*Gopherus agassizi*), which is in wide use by the Hopis today.

The painted turtle is considered a perfectly acceptable item of food, although there is no evidence for or against this use of the turtle at Awatovi.

Birds

Occasionally it is possible to check the identified birds from an archaeological site against a list of those species inhabiting the area of the site at the present time. This comparison was possible with the birds from Awatovi.

Two ornithological reports are generally regarded as standard reference works for the Hopi area. These are *Birds of the Navajo Country* (Woodbury and Russell 1945) and *Birds of the Hopi Region, Their Hopi Names and Notes on their Ecology* (Bradfield 1974). In both of these reports the authors refer to identifications of birds from Awatovi made by Glover Allen at the Museum of Comparative Zoology at Harvard University and by L.L. Hargrave. A list was also published for Awatovi by Hargrave (1939). In all instances the identifications of the various species of birds made by these men were supported by additional material from the Awatovi bone collections. However, the material on which they based their determinations was not located in the Awatovi collections that were obtained in 1974 from the Peabody Museum of Archaeology and Ethnology nor is its present whereabouts known. Perhaps it was incorporated with the osteological collections that these workers used, as this was a common practice several decades ago.

Since I have the entire faunal collection from the Awatovi excavations, excepting these first recordings of bird bones, I think it important to note this discrepancy in the location of identified materials in the event that other research workers might wish to pursue further the study of birds from Awatovi.

The paucity of small passerines and other minute birds from Awatovi may lead to false assumptions in regard to their lack of importance to the occupants of Awatovi. Only one small bird bone, a humerus of a mourning dove (*Zenaidura macroura*) was recovered, but this may have been due to the sharp sight of a particular collector. Certainly the Kiva mural decorations at Awatovi (Smith and Ewing 1952) indicate the importance of several small birds, including warblers, a magpie, a roadrunner, a woodpecker, swallows, and swifts as well as jays, blackbirds, rockwrens, and martins. The martins and the swallows and swifts have skeletons composed of minute elements and only the finer screening techniques would allow for their recovery if in fact their fragile bones survived the ravages of the extremes of heat and cold common to Antelope Mesa. There was a notable absence of all small forms in the recovered bones. J.A. Lancaster and Watson Smith both related to me that no screens were used in the excavations at Awatovi (personal communication, May 1975). A concentrated effort was not made to retrieve minute specimens. I report this fact not to indicate a fault with the excavating procedures of that time but rather to suggest a plausible reason for the lack of birds and other small vertebrates from the faunal materials that were examined.

Fortunately, the osteological collections available to me for comparison with the excavated bones were quite adequate, and identifications, where there was any doubt, could be closely checked with a series of skeletons of the species under consideration.

Taxonomic Classification of Indigenous Birds

Podicipediformes
    Podicipedidae
        Podiceps caspicus, Eared Grebe
Pelecaniformes
    Pelecanidae
        Pelecanus erythrorhynchos, White pelican
Ciconiiformes
    Ardeidae
        Ardea herodias, Great Blue Heron
Anseriformes
    Anatidae
        Branta canadensis, Canada Goose
        Anas discors, Blue-winged Teal
        Anas cyanoptera, Cinnamon Teal
Falconiformes
    Cathartidae
        Cathartes aura, Turkey Vulture
    Accipitridae
        Accipiter cooperii, Cooper's Hawk
        Circus cyaneus, Marsh Hawk

Buteo regalis, Ferruginous Hawk
Buteo jamaicensis, Red-tailed Hawk
Buteo swainsoni, Swainson's Hawk
Aquila chrysaëtos, Golden Eagle
Falco mexicanus, Prairie Falcon
Falco sparverius, Sparrow Hawk
Galliformes
    Meleagrididae
        Meleagris gallopavo, Turkey
Gruiformes
    Gruidae
        Grus canadensis, Sandhill Crane
Columbiformes
    Columbidae
        Zenaidura macroura, Mourning Dove
Strigiformes
    Strigidae
        Otus flameolus, Flammulated Owl
        Otus asio, Screech Owl
        Bubo virginianus, Great Horned Owl
        Asio otus, Long-eared Owl
Passeriformes
    Corvidae
        Corvus corax, Raven

EARED GREBE, *Podiceps caspicus*

This bird is a fairly common transient statewide. At present, it winters in small numbers in the lower Colorado and Salt River valleys. Identified from an adult left ulna, burned. Recovered from 50 - 100 cm level in room 4 of test 22. Level dated by ceramics, Pueblo V, seventeenth century.

WHITE PELICAN, *Pelecanus erythrorhynchos*

A regular transient, wintering and summering in small numbers along the lower Colorado River. Sighted on a reservoir at Kayenta in 1934. Also reported on the Little Colorado near Winslow. Represented by the proximal end of a left humerus, cut off for a bone tube or bead. Provenience unknown.

GREAT BLUE HERON, *Ardea herodias*

At present found throughout the state in small numbers. Reported in Hopi region near Moenkopi Wash and at Oraibi as recently as 1972. Identified from the distal one-half of a right radius of an adult. From the 0 - 50 cm level of room 529. Ceramics date this level as Pueblo V, seventeenth century. It is likely that wing feathers of this bird were sought after for ceremonial use, as they are in areas where the bird is more common.

CANADA GOOSE, *Branta canadensis*

At present winters in southwestern and central Arizona. It is an uncommon migrant in northern Arizona. Observed in Betatakin Canyon. An adult furculum from the Central Plaza and an adult left humerus represented by the proximal and distal ends, perhaps indicating that the shaft was used for a bone tube or bead. This animal would have been valued for both its feathers and as an item of food, as well as a source of bone for artifacts.

BLUE-WINGED TEAL, *Anas discors*

A spring transient throughout the state. Observed near Keams Canyon and from a pond north of Moenkopie. Identified from a complete right ulna from the 100 - 150 cm level of room 403. Ceramics date this level as Pueblo V, seventeenth century.

CINNAMON TEAL, *Anas cyanoptera*

Common migrant in spring. Reported from near Bluff on the San Juan River and in marshes near Tuba City and near New Oraibi. A right humerus collected from 0 - 50 cm level in room 495. Ceramic date for this level, Pueblo V, seventeenth century. Both of these brightly colored ducks would be a source of feathers for decoration. Duck feathers are used by the present day Hopi in ceremonies associated with rain. However duck feathers are not worn by the Duck Kachina (Smith and Ewing 1952, pp. 181-182).

TURKEY VULTURE, *Cathartes aura*

A common resident throughout the Hopi mesas. Identified from an adult mandible and the distal one-half of a right radius. From 100 - 150 cm level of room 3 of test 19. Unassigned date.

COOPER'S HAWK, *Accipiter cooperii*

Nests throughout the state. A summer resident which breeds on mesa tops and canyon heads. Observed on Black Mesa and from near Ganado and St. Michaels. Identified from an adult right radius from the 100 - 150 cm level of room 4 of test 22. Level dated by ceramics, Pueblo V, seventeenth century. This and the following four large species of hawks were most likely obtained for arm-band decoration in the Kachina ceremonies. Hawks are also depicted in the mural paintings and used in the Hopi Soyal and Powamu ceremonies.

MARSH HAWK, *Circus cyaneus*

At present a migrant and winter resident in the Hopi area. Sighted near Oraibi and near Chinle as well as between Kayenta and Tuba City. Identified from the distal end of a right femur from the 15 - 50 cm level of room 427, dated Pueblo V, seventeenth century.

FERRUGINOUS HAWK, *Buteo regalis*

A permanent resident and breeder in the Hopi mesa area. Common at Keams Canyon. One of the commonest hawks recovered from the excavations at Awatovi. At least fourteen individuals, including one associated skeleton, were identified. These were found in rooms 410, 456, 493, 498, 614, and 773, and test 14, room 6; test 19, room 3;, test 51, room 8; Square I of the 500 series. Remains were found from zero level through 200 cm. Ceramic dates of levels range from Pueblo IV, seventeenth century. All portions of the skeleton were represented. The proximal and distal ends of a humerus showing evidence of having been cut to free the shaft for use as a bone tube or bead was collected but not indicated as to provenience.

RED-TAILED HAWK, *Buteo jamaicensis*

As with the ferruginous hawk this species is also a permanent resident of the Hopi area. Thirty individuals were identified from throughout the excavations. Bones were recovered from rooms 403, 489, 614, 620, 625, 630, and 809. Also from test 14, rooms 5 and 6; and tests 19, room 3; test 22, rooms 1, 2, and 5; test 42, room 1 and Square K of 500 series. Several limb and pelvic fragments were collected on the floor of Kiva II. Nearly all elements of the skeletons were represented. Ceramic dates for the levels, ranging from zero to 250 cm, are Pueblo IV, seventeenth century.

SWAINSON'S HAWK, *Buteo swainsoni*

Recorded as a sparse summer resident for the Hopi region. A partial cranium was recovered from room 620 from the 50 - 100 cm level. Ceramic dates place this occupation level as Pueblo V, seventeenth century.

GOLDEN EAGLE, *Aquila chrysaëtos*

Presently a sparse permanent resident of the area. As expected, it was fairly common among the recovered bird bones. About thirty individuals were recorded from numerous rooms and levels. These range from rooms 403, 415, 419, 429, 456, 464, 478, 498, 620, 621, 624, 626, 709, 716, 733, 757, 759, and 770 and test 19, room 3; test 22, rooms 2 and 5, test 28, room 1; and Squares G and H of the 500 series. A worked adult left humerus, proximal end, was recovered from Kiva VII. Several bones exhibited butcher marks probably from disarticulating the wings for use as tool sources. Several wing bones indicate their use as a source of bone tubes or beads. A few terminal phalanges or claws (fig. 3, H) were also recovered but none were drilled for suspension. Dates from ceramics for the various levels from which golden eagle remains were collected range from Pueblo IV, seventeenth century. All portions of the skeleton were represented in the collection.

PRAIRIE FALCON, *Falco mexicanus*

Records show this bird to be a sparse permanent resident of the area. There is a representation on one of the Kiva walls that appears to be of a falcon. A right carpometa-

carpus from room 296 AA, 125 - 175 cm level in the Western Mound is the oldest recovered bird remains from Awatovi. Ceramics date this level as Pueblo III. From room 620, 50 - 100 cm level, a partial skeleton of this bird was recovered. The level is dated as Pueblo IV, seventeenth century.

SPARROW HAWK, *Falco sparverius*

Common permanent resident of the area. Identified from room 272, 100 - 150 cm in the Western Mound. Ceramics date this level as Pueblo IV. A single partial tibiotarsus was collected. From test 19, room 3, 50 - 100 cm level, an adult sternum and right femur were recovered. Ceramics date this find as Pueblo IV.

TURKEY, *Meleagris gallopavo*

The wild turkey of Arizona is an indigenous bird and was domesticated throughout the pueblo area long before the first Spanish explorers visited the Hopi mesas. There seems to be little doubt that the bird was kept by the Hopis, but if it were of prime importance this is not reflected in the numbers of individuals that were tabulated for Awatovi. In all, nine birds were collected from rooms 296 and 716; test 19, room 3; test 27, room 3; test 28, room 1; and Kivas I, II, and VII. Nearly all portions of the skeleton were represented. One humerus had been broken and regrown. There is a common practice among animal collectors who snare macaws, to break the wings of captured birds in a flock so that they cannot fly while the other birds are rounded up. The wing bones grow back together while the bird is caged but are quite deformed. I have noted this occurrence of broken bones in zoo specimens of macaws and have also seen this breakage in the humeri of other Southwestern turkeys. It is of course speculation that this same practice was carried on by Southwestern Indians. Ceramic dates for levels ranging from 45 to 250 cm are Pueblo III (for room 296) to Pueblo V, seventeenth century.

SANDHILL CRANE, *Grus canadensis*

This bird was reported as being in the vicinity of Chinle in 1926. Migratory routes could be responsible for the birds being in the vicinity of Antelope Mesa. Sightings were also reported for these birds in flight over Old Oraibi. Six individuals were determined from various wing and leg elements plus fragments of sternum and pelvis. These were from rooms 1, 296, and 528. Also from rooms 3 and 6 of test 14. Several bones exhibited cut marks on the shafts of the humerus, ulna, tarsometatarsus, those of the humerus being used for bone tubes or beads. Levels range through 50 to 100 cm. Ceramics date these levels as ranging from Pueblo III (Western Mound) to Pueblo V, seventeenth century.

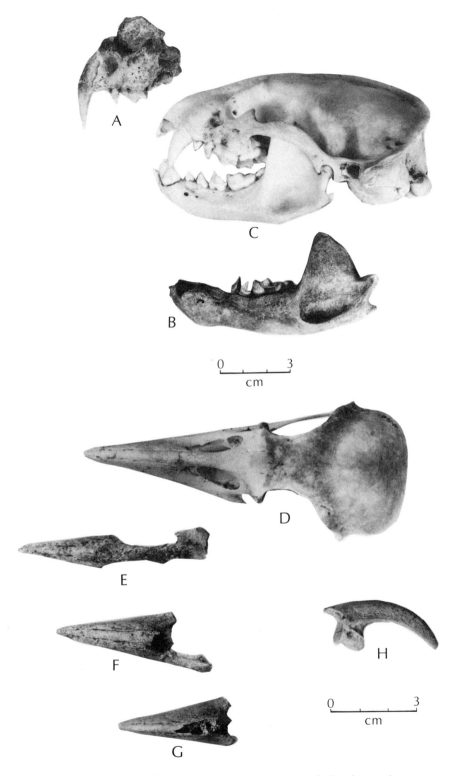

Figure 3. A, premaxilla and B, left mandible of a badger from Awatovi; C, skull and jaws of a recent example of a badger for comparison; E, F, and G, premaxillae (bills) of ravens from Awatovi; H, terminal phalanx or claw of a golden eagle from Awatovi.

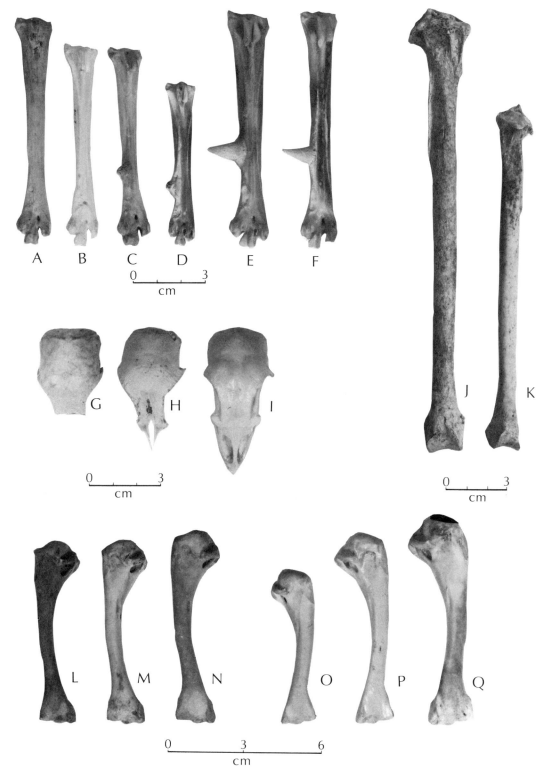

Figure 4.   A, tarsometatarsus of a domestic chicken from Awatovi; B, tarsometatarsus of recent domestic chicken (leghorn); C, tarsometatarsus of domestic chicken, with spur, from Awatovi; D, tarsometatarsus of a recent chicken (bantam); E, tarsometatarsus of a recent domestic chicken with spur (large gamecock); F, tarsometatarsus of recent domestic chicken, with spur (Old English gamecock); G, cranium of a domestic chicken from Awatovi; H, cranium of a recent domestic chicken (bantam); I, skull of recent domestic chicken (bantam); J, tibiotarsus of large form of turkey from Awatovi; K, tibiotarsus of smaller form of turkey from Awatovi; L, M, and N, humeri of domestic chickens from Awatovi; O, humerus of recent domestic chicken (bantam); P and Q, humeri of recent domestic chickens (leghorns).

MOURNING DOVE, *Zenaidura macroura*

Common summer resident of the area. A right humerus from room 471, 100 - 150 cm, was the only element of this bird recovered. It was also the smallest bird bone collected. Ceramics date this level as Pueblo V, seventeenth century.

The owls were rather well represented at Awatovi. The use of owl feathers by the Zuni to bring rain is documented (Smith and Ewing 1952, p. 173). The Hopi use owl feathers for the Soyal and Powamu ceremonies.

FLAMMULATED OWL, *Otus flammeolus*

Generally this owl occurs in the pine forest on the higher mountains of the area. A right carpometacarpus was identified but without provenience data.

SCREECH OWL, *Otus asio*

Rare in the area. Reported from near Oraibi. The proximal half of a right ulna was recovered from room 428, 0 - 50 cm level. A right radius and ulna were collected from room 3 of test 19, 0 - 50 cm. Ceramics date these specimens as Pueblo IV, seventeenth century.

GREAT HORNED OWL, *Bubo virginianus*

Permanent resident throughout the area. Twelve individuals were identified from a variety of proveniences from rooms 24, 296, 410, 618, 620, and 623. Also rooms 4 and 6 from test 14; room 3, test 22; room 1, test 28 and room 8, test 51. Wing and leg bones were represented. Two tibiotarsi had evidence of butchering on the condyles. Ceramics date these bones as occurring from Pueblo III (Western Mound) to Pueblo V, seventeenth century.

LONG-EARED OWL, *Asio otus*

Permanent resident of thick brush and woodland. A proximal end of a right humerus from room 296, AAA, 200 - 255 cm of the Western Mound is dated from Pueblo III. A right carpometacarpus from room 3, test 19, 50 - 100 cm, and a right ulna from room 2, test 22, 0 - 50 cm, are all that were recovered from this interesting little owl. The latter specimens date Pueblo IV, seventeenth century.

RAVEN, *Corvus corax*

A common permanent resident throughout the region. No less than fifty individual birds were recorded from various levels and rooms throughout Awatovi. Six rooms in the 400 series, 5 rooms in the 500 series, 9 rooms in the 600 series, 5 rooms in the 700 series, and examples from

most of the tests, too numerous to record, all produced raven bones. These date in age from Pueblo V, seventeenth century. A number of premaxillae (bills) were recovered (fig. 3, E-G). This portion of the skull would be left on the bird if it were processed to be used as a skin. They may also have been removed for attachments to sticks or wands for ceremonial use. The Hopi believe that the raven connotes death and its feathers are used in burial ceremonies (Smith and Ewing 1952, p. 181). Some wing elements exhibited cut marks most likely caused by disarticulating those members. Nearly all portions of the raven skeleton were represented in the bone collections from Awatovi.

Although psittacidine remains have been found in numerous Southwestern sites not a single bone of either the macaws (*Ara spp*) or the thick-billed parrot (*Rhynchopsitta pachyrhyncha*) was encountered in the Awatovi excavations. This is a bit puzzling in light of the rather detailed depiction of macaws on the Awatovi Kiva murals (Smith and Ewing 1952) and their use on masks and prayer sticks.

DOMESTIC CHICKEN, *Gallus gallus*

The only introduced domestic bird identified from Awatovi is of this common barnyard fowl. The turkey is, of course, a domesticated indigenous bird.

There are numerous races of domestic chickens that could possibly be represented by the remains found at Awatovi. The Mediterranean fowl include the Italian breeds of ancona, voldarno, polverara, padovana, and the leghorn. These are relatively small birds, when compared with those from Asia, and weigh from five pounds in a cock to three pounds in a pullet. Spanish breeds are for the most part the same general type as the Italian breeds but are a bit larger. The six most popular are castilian, black spanish, minorca, andalusian, barbezieux, and prat. Among the oldest breeds is the castilian. The minorca has generally been the most popular. These heavier birds range in weight from nine pounds in a cock to about six pounds in a pullet. Lastly, there is the possibility that some of the vast array of Asia short-legged bantam "game fowl," used in cock fighting, may also have found their way to Awatovi. Large spur size in comparison to a relatively small tarsometatarsus at least suggests this possibility (fig. 4).

It is interesting to note that R.G. Montgomery in his analytical restoration of the appearance of Awatovi during the height of Spanish occupation mentions the courtyard as probably having "chickens of Castille" present (Montgomery, Smith, and Brew 1949, p. 210). Unfortunately, no documentation is given for his correct assignment of a breed of chicken that was most likely present in the Spanish area.

The Mammalian Fauna

Wild as well as domestic animals were utilized by both the Spanish and Indian inhabitants of Awatovi. It is difficult at times to determine the relative importance of these two groups of animals and also of one species of an animal when compared to another within each of these groups. The faunal list that follows differs somewhat from that presented by Barbara Lawrence (1951). This is due in part to the more complete analysis undertaken for this report as compared to a select sampling as reported by Ms. Lawrence. Where there was some doubt as to whether an animal was in reality present at Awatovi, it was not carried over in this faunal list. As an example, this policy was followed in relation to material that was earlier listed as representing bison. Although Ms. Lawrence carried the listing of *Bison bison* without question under "Mammals Identified" (p. 3, 1951), she does question its presence in the accompanying text (ibid.). All fragments labeled "*Bison*" were reexamined and were deemed as undiagnostic scraps that were well within the size range of a large bovid such as the ox (*Bos taurus*). No elements were found that could positively be assigned to *Bison*. The listing of *Bison bison* has subsequently been dropped from the list of animals identified from Awatovi. Numerous complete, diagnostic bones of the domestic cow (*Bos taurus*) were identified from the recovered bones from Awatovi.

INDIGENOUS MAMMALS AT AWATOVI

Although the International Code of Zoological Nomenclature specifies the rules under which taxonomic names are to be assigned to various genera and species of animals, considerable discrepancies still exist. At times these differences, although correctly used, only add to the confusion. For example, the correct generic name for both the white-tailed and the mule deer is *Dama*. This is established by the rules of priority of naming although many vertebrate specialists still refer to this genus as *Odocoileus* due to the long years of the use of this name. The same situation exists for the rock squirrel. This animal is a member of the genus *Spermophilus*, but again common use has ingrained the name as *Citellus*. Since this compilation is in essence an archaeological report, to be used primarily by archaeologists, I have taken taxonomic liberties for which I ask the indulgence of my purist colleagues in taxonomy. Rather than refer to the huge and expensive mammal reports by Hall and Kelson (1959), which most archaeologists will not have available, I have followed the smaller and more readily accessible systematic listing put forth in Cockrum's (1960) *The Recent Mammals of Arizona*.

The purist can easily substitute any taxonomy he wishes for that put forth in Cockrum's work.

Taxonomic Classification of Indigenous Mammals

Lagomorpha
    Leporidae
        Lepus californicus, Black-tailed Jackrabbit
        Sylvilagus auduboni, Desert Cottontail
Rodentia
    Sciuridae
        Cynomys gunnisoni, White-tailed Prairie Dog
        Citellus variegatus, Rock Squirrel
        Citellus leucurus, White-tailed Antelope Squirrel
    Geomyidae
        Thomomys bottae, Valley Pocket Gopher
    Heteromyidae
        Dipodomys ordii, Ord's Kangaroo Rat
    Catoridae
        Castor canadensis, Beaver
    Cricetidae
        Onychomys leucogaster, Northern Grasshopper Mouse
        Peromyscus maniculatus, Deer Mouse
        Neotoma albigula, White-throated Woodrat
    Erethizontidae
        Erethizon dorsatum, Porcupine
Carnivora
    Canidae
        Canis latrans, Coyote

Canis familiaris, Small and Large Pueblo Dogs
      Urocyon cinereoargenteus, Gray Fox
Ursidae
      Euarctus americanus, Black Bear
Mustelidae
      Taxidea taxus, Badger
Felidae
      Felis concolor, Mountain Lion
      Lynx rufus, Bobcat
Artiodactyla
      Cervidae
          Odocoileus hemionus, Mule Deer
      Antilocapridae
          Antilocapra americana, Pronghorned Antelope
      Bovidae
          Ovis canadensis, Desert Big-horned Sheep

BLACK-TAILED JACKRABBIT, *Lepus californicus*
and
DESERT COTTONTAIL, *Sylvilagus auduboni*

Without a doubt the commonest, most numerous remains of indigenous mammals at Awatovi. Of the hundreds of rooms that were excavated nearly all had remains of both forms. An example of an average occurrence of these animals and their importance as a food source may be found in room 5 of test 14 dated as Pueblo IV by ceramics. A total of 214 bones representing 7 jackrabbits and 43 bones representing 4 cottontails were recovered from the bone accumulation of this one room. Since 90 percent of the non-Spanish portion of the site has yet to be excavated, a minimal count of these animals based on the 10 percent of the rooms examined would be of dubious value. However, the relative importance of these two animals, to each other as well as to other food animals that were procured, will be discussed in a selected sampling of rooms exhibiting a cultural change through time. The importance of these two animals as a staple food was due in part to their abundance but also partly to the ability of young and old members of the community to obtain them for food. Rabbit sticks, particularly from the Hopi area, are among the oldest game-getting devices of the Southwest. Early explorers to the pueblo areas refer to seeing and being offered cleaned and dried rabbits as a food source. Sun dried or "jerked" rabbit meat would certainly be easy to process and store for leaner times and it appears that a ready supply was generally at hand.

All portions of the skeletons of both jackrabbits and cottontails were present in the Awatovi collections as were both old and young individuals. A number of pointed awls had been manufactured from both the ulna and tibia of the jackrabbit. Many bones bore evidence of burning or charring.

The larger rodents probably served in one capacity or another as a supplementary food source but some, particularly the burrowers, may have been present in the rooms as intrusive forms after abandonment of the pueblo. The smaller mice may have been present in the rooms as scavangers of spilled grain or food particles. Certainly their size and numbers do not indicate a protein source of importance for the inhabitants of Awatovi.

WHITE-TAILED PRAIRIE DOG, *Cynomys gunnisoni*

Forty-one individuals were determined from rooms ranging from the earliest levels in the Western Mound through the abandonment of Awatovi. These were principally from units within the 400, 500, and 600 series of rooms. All portions of the skeletons were represented, and bones from Square F of the 500 series were burned and charred. This little rodent, although choosy as to its habitation requirements, is generally quite abundant in the areas where it establishes its colonies. The amount of edible meat from an animal that averages about two pounds in live weight is considerable. Seventy percent of this live weight, or about one and one-half pounds, is usable for food (White 1953). Field ration for a frontier military armed force in the Southwest was established as one pound of meat per man supplemented by other grain-based foods. Based on this estimate of nutritional values, one prairie dog per adult per day could provide the basic protein needed to sustain life in that area. Perhaps future excavations of the bulk of the rooms yet to be cleared will give us a better idea of the numbers of individual prairie dogs that were actually utilized during the entire occupation of Awatovi. Only a suggestion of their use, rather than proof of the importance of these small animals, can be gained from the small sample that was recovered.

ROCK SQUIRREL, *Citellus variegatus*

As with the prairie dog, this rather large squirrel is abundant in the areas it inhabits and produces over 70 percent of usable meat from a live weight of one and one-half pounds per animal. Only thirteen animals were represented by bones from rooms within the 400, 500, 600, and 700 series. Several were also collected from tests 19 and 28. Nearly all portions of the skeletons were represented. No burning or altering of these bones was noted.

WHITE-TAILED ANTELOPE SQUIRREL, *Citellus leucurus*

This chipmunk-sized little rodent was present as a single individual only from room 7, test 52. No particular importance is given to it. The subspecies of this animal, *C. l. cinnamomeus* is a common animal of the mesas today.

VALLEY POCKET GOPHER, *Thomomys bottae*

This burrower, whether intrusive or contemporary, within various levels of Awatovi is represented by five individuals. It is found at the lowest level in the Western Mound as well as in later proveniences. Only skull and

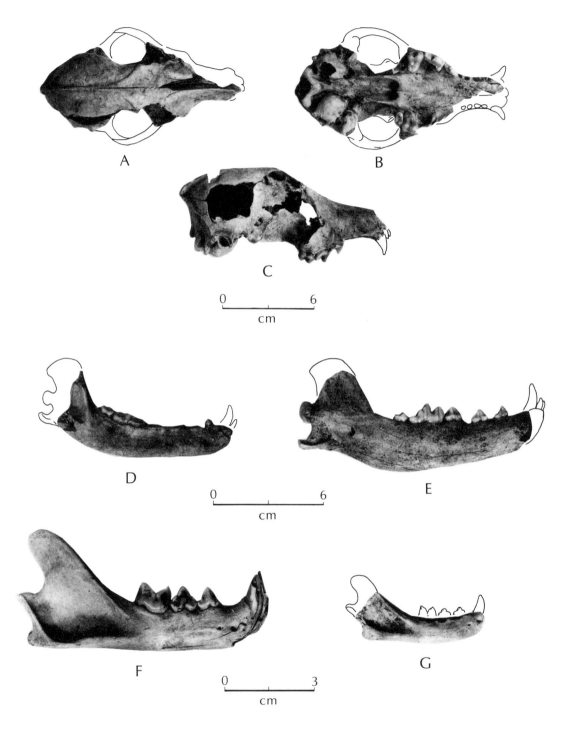

Figure 5.   A, dorsal aspect of skull of a small long-faced Pueblo Indian dog from Awatovi; B, palatal aspect and C, right lateral aspect of same skull; D, mandible of small Pueblo Indian dog; E, mandible of large Pueblo Indian dog, both from Awatovi; F, right mandible of a bobcat from Awatovi; G, right mandible of a domestic cat from Awatovi. Note: F and G are the same scale for comparison.

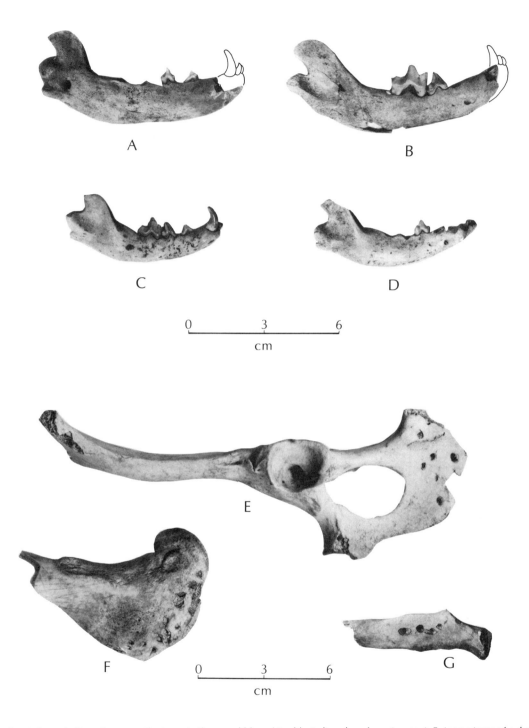

Figure 6.   A through D, various growth stages in the mandibles of Pueblo Indian dogs from Awatovi; E, innominate of a domestic sheep with tooth marks visible from young dogs living at Awatovi; F, toothmarks on the distal end of a domestic sheep femur from Awatovi; G, neural spine of a domestic sheep vertebra from Awatovi having the tooth marks of a puppy.

mandible fragments were recovered. It may be well to point out that at the University of Arizona's Archaeological Field School at the fourteenth-century Grasshopper Ruin this pocket gopher is occasionally encountered alive at depths exceeding one meter during the course of excavating. Its presence at Awatovi as a fortuitous form cannot be discounted. No evidence of altering or burning was present on the few bones of this animal that were examined.

ORD'S KANGAROO RAT, *Dipodomys ordii*

The remains of the kangaroo rat established the presence of only two individuals in the faunal materials at Awatovi. These were from room 5 of test 14 and room 3 of test 19. No significance is given them in regard to the occupants of the mission area.

BEAVER, *Castor canadensis*

In an area where the beaver is confined to the larger river drainages, it is a bit surprising that some ten individuals were identified from rooms in the 500 and 600 series, as well as from rooms 4 and 6 of test 22 and room 13 of test 51. Both mature and immature forms were present. Several had evidence of butchering present on the scapula and pelvis. A few isolated caudal vertebrae were recovered from room 631, perhaps indicating the remains of a broiled beaver tail, considered a delicacy by Anglo frontiersmen who recorded their experiences in frontier America. This food choice may have been first encountered among native American peoples.

NORTHERN GRASSHOPPER MOUSE, *Onychomys leucogaster*

The smallest mammal represented in the faunal assemblages from Awatovi are of this mouse and of the deer mouse. Only the rostral portion of one skull was collected from room 507. No cultural importance is attached to it.

DEER MOUSE, *Peromyscus maniculatus*

As with the grasshopper mouse, this small rodent is present only as a single animal, represented by lumbar, caudal, fragmentary limb, and pelvis material. It was from room 527. No importance in relation to the occupants of the room is attached to this one rodent. As with the smaller birds, perhaps the lack of any significant numbers of all small rodents is due to the methods that were used to collect vertebrates rather than to their actual absence at Awatovi.

WHITE-THROATED WOODRAT, *Neotoma albigula*

This animal is commonly referred to as a "pack rat" and its habit of carrying off numerous objects from around human occupations to its moundlike nest is well known. It is a common animal of the Hopi mesas at present. Only seven individuals were identified. They were from rooms in the 500, 600, and 700 series and from room 6, test 14; room 3, test 19, and room 4, test 22. One individual was associated with a human burial (104) in the fill of room 772. It may have been present as an intrusive form. No significance is attached to these few animals.

PORCUPINE, *Erethizon dorsatum*

This is one rodent, easy to capture despite its prickly adornment, that can supply ten pounds of usable meat from its live weight of fifteen pounds for an adult animal (White 1953). Thirty animals were determined from rooms within the 400, 500, 600, and 700 series, as well as from rooms 1, 2, 4, 6, and 7 of test 22; room 2 of test 31 and room 1 of test 42. At least seven individuals were immature animals. Nearly all portions of the skeletons were represented by the recovered bones. No evidence of butchering or burning was present on the examined specimens.

COYOTE, *Canis latrans*

Coyotes were sparse from rooms throughout the ruin from all proveniences. In many instances, it was not possible to state with certainty whether the bones collected were of coyote or domestic dog. These are indicated as *Canis sp,* domestic dog/coyote. The reason for this animal's presence at Awatovi is not explained from its bones. It is, of course, a common animal of the Hopi mesas today.

DOMESTIC DOG, *Canis familiaris*

The native Pueblo Indian domestic dog is generally assignable to three separate size categories for dogs recovered from prehistoric sites in the southwest. These categories are a large Pueblo Indian dog, a small long-faced Pueblo Indian dog, and a small short-faced Pueblo Indian dog. Both of the first two size categories are represented in the Awatovi collections. The dogs are present in the earliest proveniences of the Western Mound, where a complete skull of the large Pueblo Indian dog was recovered. This animal is about the size of the local coyote but is a bit heavier in build and has a shortened rostral area. The smaller dog (fig. 5, A-C) is about the size of a cocker spaniel (but in no way related to this American Kennel Club breed). Thirty-five individuals were determined from a number of rooms from all age proveniences. An immature individual about eight weeks old (determined by the status of the dentition) was recovered from Kiva I of room 10 in test 22. All age groups of individuals were represented (fig. 6, A-D). A continually breeding population must have been present at Awatovi during much of its occupation if we are to judge by the puppy-chewed bones that were identified (fig. 6, E-G). These were usually of the more cartilaginous portions of artiodactyl skeletons. An unusual selection of dog bones for artifact sources was noted among quite a few dog limb bones.

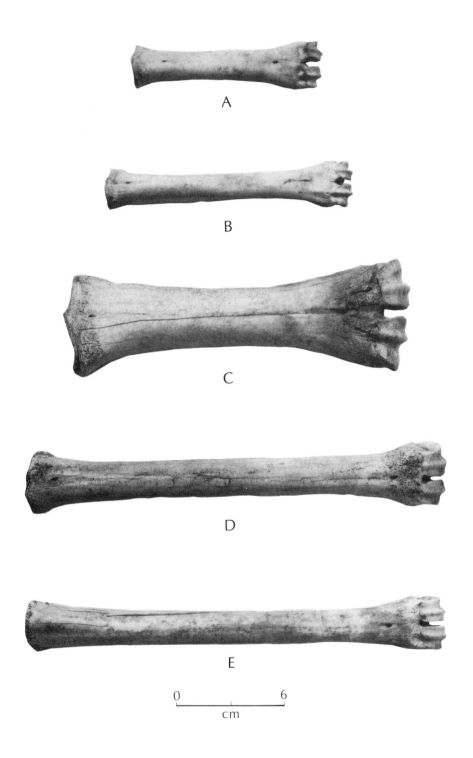

Figure 7. Differences in metapodial proportions of the common artiodactyls found at Awatovi. A, domestic goat; B, domestic sheep; C, domestic cow; D, mule deer; E, pronghorned antelope.

The proximal ends of tibiae and femora were scored and broken most likely for bone tubes or bead blanks. One distal end of a tibia had been manufactured into a pointed awl. Several vertebrae were burned or charred.

GRAY FOX, *Urocyon cinereoargenteus*

Five individuals were determined from bones from rooms in the 500 and 600 series, as well as from room 6 of test 22 and room 2 of test 38. It is possible that these animals were obtained for their skins to be used for adornment of the Kachina dancers as they are today. One femur was cut for a bone tube blank or bead.

BLACK BEAR, *Euarctos americanus*

Perhaps never a common animal in the Antelope Mesa area, it was identified from a partial femur found in room 792. Barbara Lawrence (1951, p. 3) mentions that "the only bear found was an isolated lot of terminal ungual phalanges." These would have been with the initial lot of bones that were examined by Glover Allen but, as with birds that he reported, their present whereabouts is unknown.

BADGER, *Taxidea taxus*

Since this animal would hardly be considered a food source, for the same reasons that its relatives, the skunks and weasels, are shunned, its presence in some numbers at Awatovi is a bit perplexing. The Badger Clan is still an active group on the Hopi mesas and perhaps its presence at Awatovi has to do with its ceremonial significance. Some twenty-eight animals are represented from rooms in the 400, 500, 600, 700, and 800 series. Also from rooms in test 14, 22, 31, 35, 40, 52, and 62. Nearly all portions of the skeletons were present and a considerable number of skulls and jaws (fig. 3, A-B). Several had evidence of butchering and a few bones from room 1 of test 31 were burned. A fragmentary humerus was from the ventilator shaft of a Kiva in room 11 of test 22. Both old and young animals were determined.

MOUNTAIN LION, *Felis concolor*

A metacarpal of a large adult from Section 3, Square A is all that is representative of this large cat. No significance is given this animal based on this one bone.

BOBCAT, *Lynx rufus*

As with the badger, this nonfood animal was present in considerable numbers at Awatovi. At least eighty-six individuals were present in levels dating from Pueblo IV to the abandonment of the pueblo. The rooms that produced bobcat remains were in the 400, 500, 600, 700, and 800 series as well as from tests 14, 19, 22, 24, 27, 28, 31, 38, 42, and 51. Some bones showed evidence of butchering but of a nature that could be attributed to skinning. Some few elements were charred. At least one

femur had been used as a source for a bone tube or bead (room 4, test 22). Small kittens as well as old adults were present and many jaws and skull fragments were recovered as well as other parts of the postcranial skeletons.

MULE DEER, *Odocoileus hemionus*

The remains of this animal was found in rooms of all proveniences and from all parts of the excavations. Its importance through time at Awatovi is discussed elsewhere. It is sufficient to state that it was a basic source of food at Awatovi from the earliest occupation to the abandonment of the dwellings.

PRONGHORNED ANTELOPE, *Antilocapra americana*

Although the mesa on which Awatovi is located is named for this animal, it is not present there today. The older Hopis on Second Mesa informed me that the last animal was killed in that area about the end of the second decade in this century. As with the deer its remains are too numerous to list by provenience or room. It is identified by many horn cores and some of its bones can be separated from other similarly structured artiodactyls (fig. 7, E). The size of many animals, judging by horn cores, is equal to those considered quite large by present-day standards. As with deer, they exhibit considerable evidence of butchering and many fragmentary bones are burned and charred.

DESERT BIG-HORNED SHEEP, *Ovis canadensis*

This animal, probably never common in the Hopi area, is no longer there. It was, however, common enough to be considered a game animal in the San Francisco Mountain area and to the south of Flagstaff in the late 1800s (Buechner 1960). Only fragmentary bones representing four animals were recovered from rooms 620, 621, and 788. This animal is generally difficult to separate osteologically from its domestic counterpart *Ovis aries*. The determinations were decided upon only after close comparisons with adequate skeletal material.

The four fused metapodials of artiodactyls (two metacarpals and two metatarsals for each animal) are commonly encountered in a site when little else of the skeleton is known. This is due in part to the compact structure of the fused "cannon bones" and also because these particular bones were saved as tool sources by the people of many early cultures throughout North America. Although these similar appearing bones are at times impossible to distinguish on a specific level, particularly if fragmentary, they generally have proportions and characteristics that allow for their identification when found complete (fig. 7). Unfortunately, the bulk of these elements known from Awatovi were less than complete, being instead proximal or distal condyles or the splinters from the medial portions of the shafts.

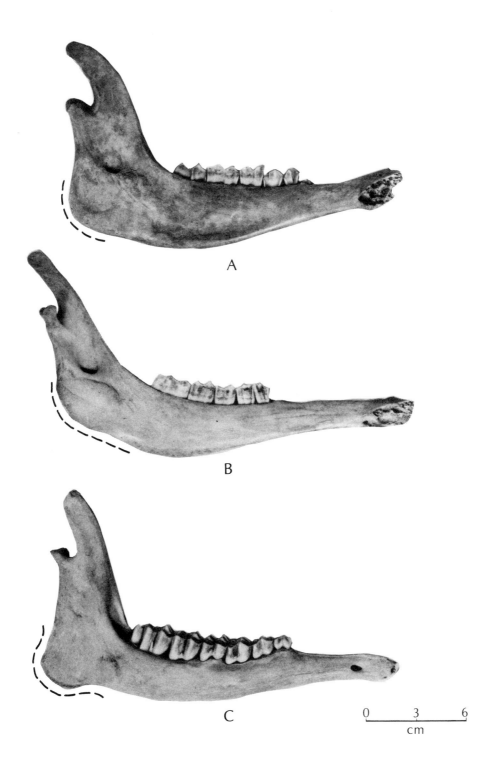

Figure 8. Left mandibles of common artiodactyls from Awatovi. A, domestic sheep; B, pronghorned antelope; C, mule deer. Note diagnostic differences in region of jaw angle.

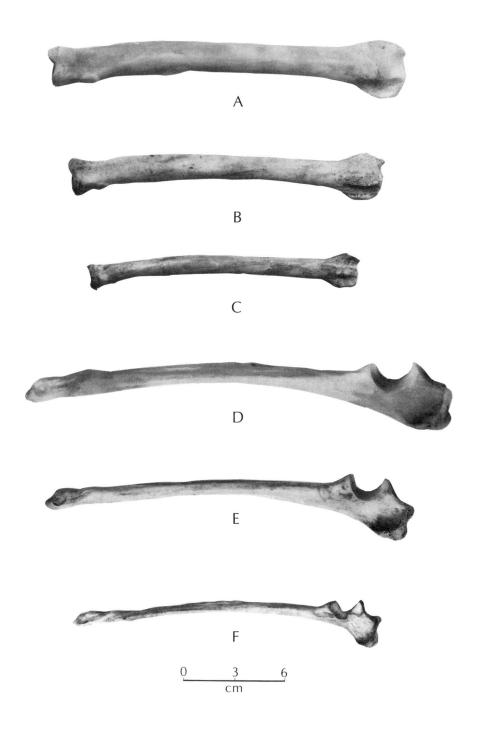

Figure 9.   A, radius and D, ulna of recent Arizona wolf; B, radius and E, ulna of Spanish greyhound from Awatovi; C, radius and F, ulna of recent Arizona coyote. The wild canids are for size comparison. The same elements from the large Pueblo dog would be smaller than those of the coyote.

The lower jaws or mandibles, although seemingly very similar in form, can be quite easily separated on tooth structure or outline of the lower margin of the ramus particularly at the angle of the jaw (fig. 8).

INTRODUCED DOMESTIC MAMMALS AT AWATOVI

Taxonomic Classification

Carnivora
        Canidae
                Canis familiaris, Spanish Greyhound
        Felidae
                Felis domesticus, Domestic Cat
Perissodactyla
        Equidae
                Equus caballus, Horse
                Equus asinus, Burro
Artiodactyla
        Suidae
                Sus scrofa, Pig
        Bovidae
                Bos taurus, Cow
                Ovis aries, Sheep
                Capra hircus, Goat

SPANISH GREYHOUND, *Canis familiaris*

Barbara Lawrence (1951) referred to some canid remains from Awatovi that were larger than the big Pueblo Indian dog but smaller than the local wolf. She regarded these as a possible hybrid or cross of the two forms. This assumption was based on only a few random selections of bones from Awatovi that were used to compile the first brief faunal analysis of the site. After lengthy examination and comparison of all the recovered bones from Awatovi, a considerable number of additional elements of this large canid have turned up. These were compared closely with similar elements found in the coyote, the large Pueblo Indian dog from Awatovi, and the local race of wolf, as well as with identified breeds of modern domestic dogs. I believe that these bones (fig. 9, B-E) represent examples of the Spanish greyhounds that were brought to this hemisphere by many early Spanish explorers. Their accounts of using these dogs to "control" the Indians that they contacted are scattered throughout the literature.

These dogs are from proveniences dated as representing ages from A.D. 1600 to 1700. The animals are larger than both the coyote and large Pueblo dogs but smaller than the local wolf. One of the more interesting aspects of future work at Awatovi would be to collect, if present, more material of this heretofore unrepresented European introduction to the southwest. More often than not large canid bones from archaeological sites are simply assumed to be wolf and are labeled and stored as such. Cranial material will, of course, disprove this categorization.

DOMESTIC CAT, *Felis domesticus*

Barbara Lawrence (1951) correctly identified this small companion of man as occurring at Awatovi but did not feel confident enough to make this statement with certainty. We were able to locate all of the original material used by Ms. Lawrence as well as a good deal of the remaining skeleton from room 505. Ceramics date the level from which the cat was collected as being Pueblo V (fig. 5, G).

This little carnivore was closely compared with all forms that it might be mistaken for, as well as with a series of domestic cat skeletons. Without a doubt it represents a small cat, belonging perhaps to a newly assigned Franciscan who wanted some link with a more leisurely life when he headed for frontier Awatovi. One can only speculate whether the arrival of the cat caused any unusual interest among the Hopis, as did Father Sagaard's cat when he took it with him among the Hurons. The Awatovi felid represents the earliest domestic cat remains recovered in the Southwest. Early felids are of course known from Colonial Williamsburg and elsewhere in the eastern United States.

DOMESTIC HORSE, *Equus caballus*
and
BURRO, *Equus asinus*

It is a matter of record that Spanish explorers to the southwest, starting with Coronado, had mules and burros in their caravans as well as riding horses. The former were generally more sure-footed on rocky terrain than were horses and adapted well to a desert environment and terrain. Mule pack trains were also used to supply the outlying Spanish missions; so there seems to be little doubt that all three equids were present at one time or another at Awatovi. Taxonomically and osteologically there is little difference between the domestic horse (*Equus caballus*) and the burro (*Equus asinus*) or for that matter the mule, which is derived from the union of a male *Equus asinus* and a female *Equus caballus*. The burro can at times be separated on its smaller sized elements. Comparably sized bones of the horse and mule can be distinguished because they would not be fully ossified. One characteristic that is present on the grinding surface pattern of the upper molars of the equids can be used to distinguish the horse from the other two animals. This character is the pli-caballan fold (fig. 10), which is visible in the infolded enamel pattern of the horse. This fold is absent in the molars of the mule and burro. Several

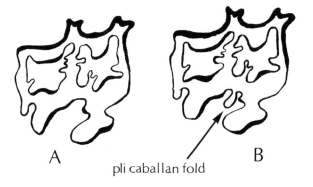

Figure 10.   Occlusal enamel pattern in upper molars of equids.
Pli-caballan fold is present in horses, absent in both
burros and mules.

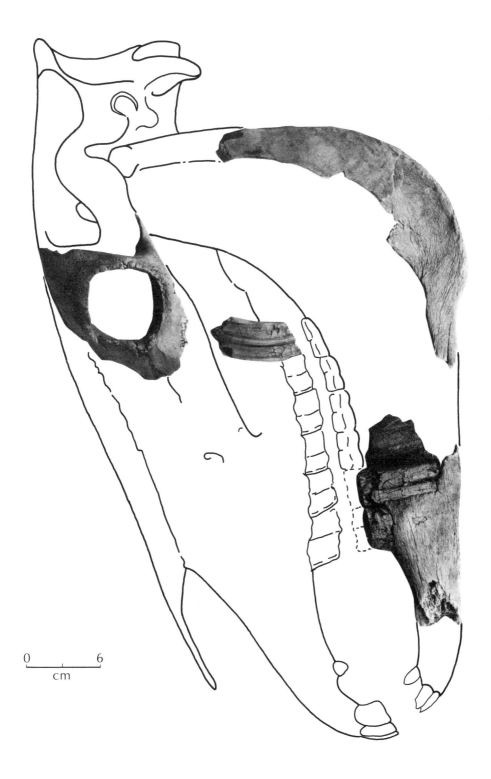

Figure 11.   Composite restoration of domestic horse skull from Awatovi.

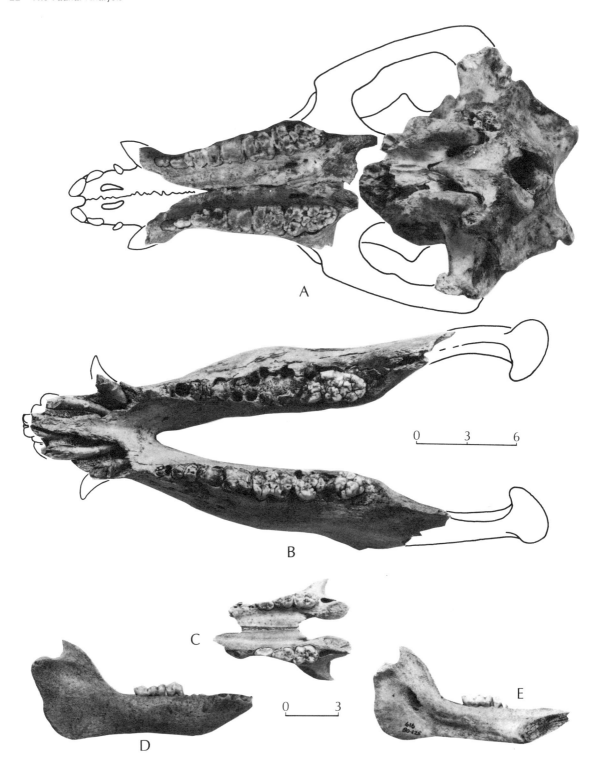

Figure 12.   A, palatal aspect of a skull of a large domestic pig from Awatovi; B, occlusal aspect of articulated lower jaws of a large
domestic pig from Awatovi; C, palate, D and E, mandibles of immature "shoats" of domestic pigs from Awatovi.

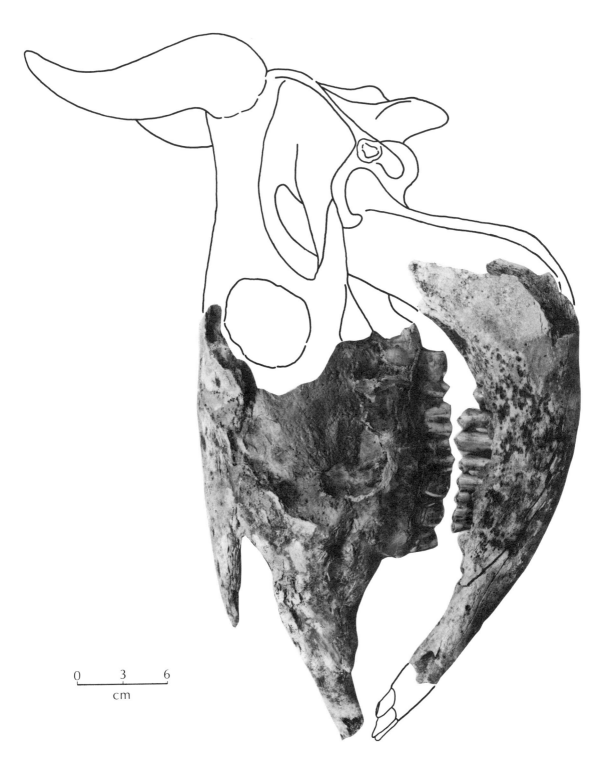

Figure 13. Composite skull of a domestic cow from Awatovi.

Figure 14.   A, left lateral and B, frontal aspects of a modern domestic sheep (ram) of mixed breed similar to those found at Awatovi; C, horn core of domestic sheep (ram) from Awatovi; D, left lateral aspect of occipital area of skull of a domestic sheep (ram), having horn core base, from Awatovi; E, frontal aspect of skull of domestic sheep (ram), having horn core bases, from Awatovi.

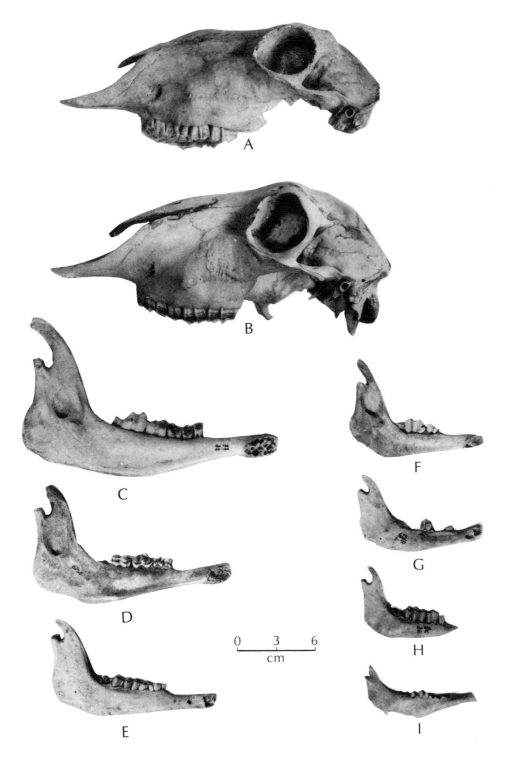

0   3   6
cm

Figure 15.   A, left lateral aspect of a skull of a domestic sheep (ewe) from Awatovi; B, left lateral aspect of a skull of a domestic sheep (ewe) which is of unknown ancestry (scrub) — from an Indian herd in Canyon de Chelly, collected in 1973 for comparison with Awatovi animals; C through I, growth stages of Awatovi domestic sheep mandibles from newborn lambs (I) through various ages (H to D) to adults (C) — all from Awatovi.

complete upper molars were present in the collections from Awatovi. All had the pli-caballan fold present indicating that they represented the horse, *Equus caballus*. Thirty-seven different occurrences of bones of the horse were identified from rooms in the 400, 500, 600, 700, and 800 series as well as from rooms in tests 22, 28, 31, 41, and 62. Several of the limb elements showed preserved evidence of butchering. Enough of the skull elements were present to give an idea of size (fig. 11). Terminal phalanges assigned to the burro were collected from rooms 757 and 760. Ceramic dates for levels containing these bones are from A.D. 1600 to 1700.

DOMESTIC PIG, *Sus scrofa*

At least eighteen individuals were identified from rooms in the 400, 500, 600, and 700 series. A number of bones had butcher marks present on the terminal or articular ends, indicating dismemberment of these elements. One does not generally associate swine raising with a desert environment such as is found in the vicinity of Awatovi. A lush woodland vegetation, where they can root among the young trees and bushes for roots, acorns, and other fodder usually found on a forest floor, is more to the liking of pigs. Dendrochronological interpretation of numerous tree-ring cores from archaeological sites on the Hopi mesas gives us some idea of the comparative wetness or dryness of northern Arizona at the time of occupation of Spanish Awatovi. Dr. J.S. Dean, of the Tree Ring Laboratory at the University of Arizona, informed me that Awatovi during the last half of the seventeenth century was comparatively wet (personal communication June 20, 1975). It is worth noting that apparently successful pig farming is carried out on a rather large scale, in a similar environment to Awatovi's, at Snowflake, Arizona, one hundred miles to the south of Antelope Mesa.

The pigs recovered from Awatovi range in size from small shoats to a large individual whose skull corresponded closely to the skull of a 400-pound individual (fig. 12).

DOMESTIC COW, *Bos taurus*

The bones, representing fifty individuals, were identified from rooms in the 400, 500, 600, 700, and 800 series as well as from rooms in tests 22, 31, 48, 50, 51, and 62. Bones were also received from Kiva fill in room 844 and from Kiva VII. In figure 15, page 77 of the Franciscan Awatovi Report (Montgomery, Smith, and Brew 1949) and in the accompanying text referring to this illustration, a horse skull is indicated as being in the fill between the bottom of the floor of room 453 in Church II and the top of a kiva wall underlying this room floor. Fortunately, this specimen had been well tagged and was located in the faunal collections sent from Harvard University to the

University of Arizona for study. In reality the specimen is the anterior portion of the left side of a skull, with cheek teeth, of a domestic cow, *Bos taurus* (fig. 13). Both young and old individuals are present and many elements of the postcranial skeletons are preserved; many had evidence of butchering on the bones. The individuals range from specimens that compared well with skeletons of animals having a known weight of 1,200 pounds to larger-sized individuals that might be mistaken for buffalo (*Bison bison*). These latter, however, I believe represent oxen that would be commonly used as beasts of burden at a settlement such as Franciscan Awatovi.

DOMESTIC SHEEP, *Ovis aries*
and
DOMESTIC GOAT, *Capra hircus*

As stated elsewhere, these two similarly structured animals cannot generally be separated unless a large skeletal collection of both forms is available for comparison or unless there is a comparative study of the local forms available for use. Neither of these conditions could be applied to the Awatovi sheep and goats. In particular instances, as with the lower limb bones, (fig. 7) or with the skull and horn core fragments (fig. 1, 14, 15) specific identifications could be arrived at. In recent years there have been several publications designed to facilitate the identification and separation of bones of domestic sheep (*Ovis aries*) from those of the similar appearing domestic goat (*Capra hircus*). Foremost among these manuals is the German publication by Boessneck, Müller, and Teichert (1964). However, it was pointed out at a symposium on zooarchaeology held at the fortieth annual meeting of the Society for American Archaeology in Dallas, that these characteristics may vary considerably from one geographic area to another. Joachim Boessneck, a participant at the 1975 symposium, agreed that his monograph, based on Old World forms, may have limited value when applied to sheep and goats from other parts of the world.

A number of outside forces apparently influence the growth of subtle morphological features that are used to separate these closely related animals. Certainly climate, type of terrain, and differing diet are known to affect bone growth. Not enough information is available at present to predict to what degree these differing forces change the osteological characters of bone.

In the following discussion of the sheep and goats, I have categorized bones that are questionable to any degree as representing sheep/goat. Where specific assignments can be arrived at (some horn cores in particular) they are designated as such. Comparisons of numbers of positively identified domestic sheep (*Ovis aries*) with those of positively identified domestic goats (*Capra hircus*) indicate a considerable majority of sheep from the earliest Spanish occupation to the abandonment of

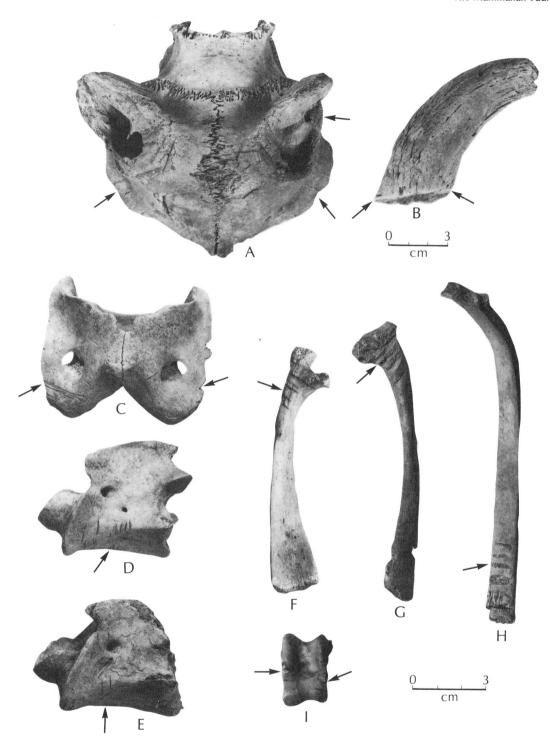

Figure 16.   Evidence of butchering on artiodactyl bones from Awatovi. A, fragmentary domestic sheep skull with evidence of the horn cores having been sawed off; B, domestic sheep horn core (ram) with saw cut base; C, atlas with knife cuts; D and E, cervical vertebrae with knife cuts on centra; F, G, and H, ribs with hack or chop marks visible; I, astragalus with knife cuts visible from either butchering or skinning. Arrows indicate evidence of butchering.

Awatovi. All age groups from newborn lambs to old individuals were present from all levels and from most rooms in all series (fig. 15). Their relative importance to other fauna is discussed elsewhere. All parts of the skeletons were present and many bones, particularly the cervical vertebrae (fig. 16, C-E) and the ribs (fig. 16, F-H) and limb elements (fig. 16-I), showed evidence of cutting or hacking. Much of this work suggested less than skill from the meat cutters.

The churro or common sheep of Spain is often referred to as being the dominant breed brought to New Spain by the early explorers and settlers of that country. This animal has been described as being scrawny and long-legged and needing little care, but with straight wool that was almost greaseless and could be woven without washing (Underhill 1956). This sheep was a product of the dry desert country and had grazed on the uplands of Spain for centuries before coming to America. Arizona terrain was probably much like its home territory. The other popular Spanish breed of sheep was the Merino, a breed that also had its early roots in the hot deserts of Africa and was suited to the southwestern United States. It was an animal possessing finer wool than the churro and in Spain was reserved for the use of the nobility. It is doubtful if many or any of this breed found their way to Awatovi.

It is not conceivable that only purebred animals were sent to Spanish colonial outposts. More often than not mixed breeds or those animals whose breeding records and origins are not known were the ones sent to the frontier missions such as Awatovi. An animal of this unknown lineage is termed a "scrub" by stock breeders. Such a "scrub" was collected in 1973 in the Canyon de Chelly area, to the east of Awatovi. The skull of this mixed breed compares very well with one from Awatovi (fig. 15). The fragmentary skulls with horn cores and the separated horn cores of sheep that were collected from Awatovi are quite similar to Spanish breeds of sheep today that have horns that curve forward behind the ears and are rather close to the head (fig. 14). The ewes are hornless. The goats from Awatovi (fig. 1) are indistinguishable from the scimitar-horned goats of the *Capra hircus aegagrus* group. This group of goats is native to range country in Asia that is craggy and rocky, with an environment not unlike that found in the Hopi mesa country. The goats at Awatovi may have been brought there by the Franciscans to fill a need for fresh dairy products. Goats can furnish dairy products while grazing on land too poor for cattle. A goat can produce from two to three quarts of milk daily and can supply that amount over a seven to ten month period (Briggs 1970).

By the amount of butchering evidence on the bones of both sheep and goats and from the examples of burned and charred elements, it seems likely that these small artiodactyls also filled in as a supplement to the usual deer and antelope.

CHANGE IN FAUNAL SELECTION THROUGH TIME

Although the Spanish construction area of the three churches and the post-1680 Hopi additions were fully excavated, only about 10 percent of the defined habitation area of Awatovi has been dug (fig. 17, 18). With these facts in mind, I believe that a minimum faunal count, or even a percentage comparison, of the excavated material to date would have little actual meaning. The approach that does have some validity is a comparison of samples from three separate cultural areas to determine to some extent a difference in faunal selection through time, due to cultural influence. The earliest habitation area at Awatovi is the Western Mound, entirely pre-Hispanic in age. The rooms from this area are in the 200 and 300 series. Rooms in the 500 and 600 series in the units north of Church II have been dated by ceramics as being occupied between Pueblo IV and the beginning of the eighteenth century (A.D. 1300 - 1700). By analyzing the bones from the 0 - 50 cm layer, I assume that they better represent the time of the Spanish occupation. There is no way of separating the time period between A. D. 1680 and the abandonment of the pueblo in A. D. 1701. The rooms occupied during the postrebellion period can be defined within the church, owing to a change in form and structure between the original Spanish walls and the Hopi additions of post-1680. These rooms are in the 400 and 700 series. One troubling fact kept emerging during this comparison of different occupation levels. All of the units at Awatovi were built upon the debris of previous Hopi occupations. There is no way to determine to what extent mixing of fauna occurred, because of earlier diggers, before the Harvard crew started excavating in 1935.

Published carbon 14 dates for Awatovi were for the most part unsatisfactory for establishing close dates for various units. These dates were generally obtained from loose charcoal within various rooms rather than from rafters or beams that were in place in the walls. Very few had the outer growth rings present necessary to determine the date of cutting. Ceramics were better suited for general dating, and I have relied rather heavily on this means of arriving at occupation dates for various rooms.

It was not feasible, under present circumstances, to tabulate and compare all the bones from all of the hundreds of rooms that were excavated. Instead, I selected a sampling of a number of rooms from each of the three major cultural change areas and have compared the data from these. One must remember that the bones were collected more than forty years ago, and data that are recorded at excavations today were not tabulated at that time. Lengthy correspondence with existing members of the expedition to resolve some of these problems, for the most part, left the questions unanswered.

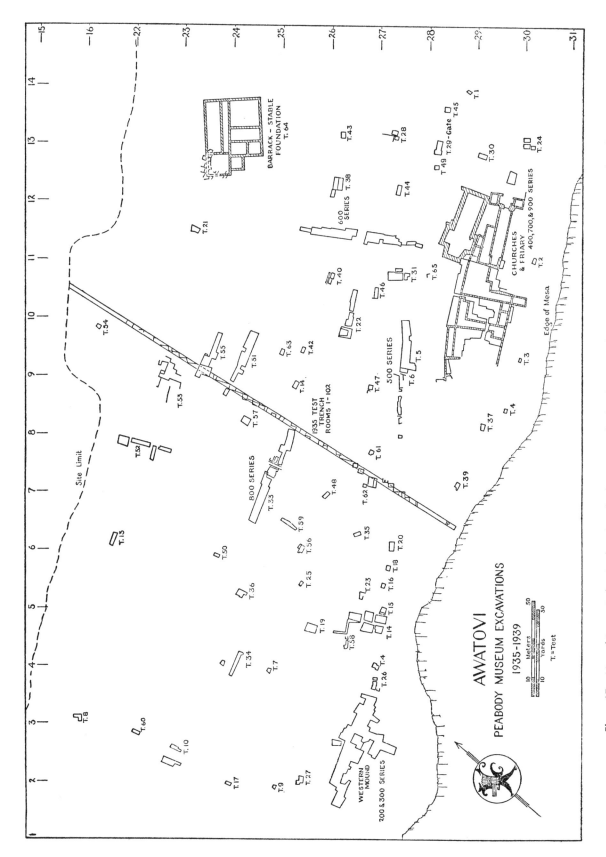

Figure 17. Map of Awatovi, showing location of Indian-occupied cultural units in relation to Spanish structures. Note numbered room units in series, referred to in text.

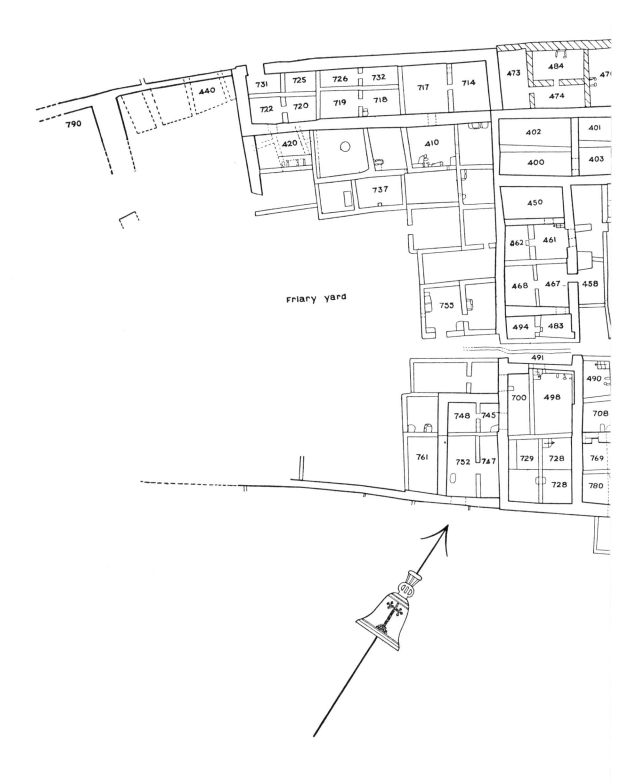

PRE-HISPANIC OCCUPATION
OF WESTERN MOUND

Pueblo III to Early Pueblo IV, A. D. 1100 - 1450, fauna from rooms 203, 207, 220, 222, 230, 236, 243, 245, 249, 272, and 296.

Taxonomic List

Indigenous Animals	Percentage
Lepus californicus, Black-tailed Jackrabbit	31.8
Sylvilaqus auduboni, Desert Cottontail	30.3
Citellus variegatus, Rock Squirrel	1.5
Cynomys gunnisoni, White-tailed Prairie Dog	9.0
Thomomys bottae, Valley Pocket Gopher	3.0
Peromyscus maniculatus, Deer Mouse	1.5
Canis familiaris, Domestic Dog	1.5
Canis sp., Domestic Dog/Coyote	1.5
Odocoileus hemionus, Mule Deer	4.5
Odocoileus/Antilocapra, Deer/Antelope	6.0
Falco mexicanus, Prairie Falcon	3.0
Meleagris gallopavo, Turkey	1.5
Grus canadensis, Sandhill Crane	1.5
Bubo virginianus, Great Horned Owl	1.5
Asio otus, Long-eared Owl	1.5
Total	99.6

As with other Southwestern sites of comparable age, the basic food source appears to be black-tailed jackrabbit and desert cottontail, followed by deer and antelope. Many of the examined bones of this latter group were of those portions of the skeleton where it is not possible to state with certainty whether they represent deer or antelope. The same osteological similarity exists between many of the postcranial elements of domestic dogs and coyotes. This questionable status has been indicated in the taxonomic listing. Awatovi differed in one respect that was quite noticeable when compared with other sites of the same age from the Southwest. This was the paucity of turkey remains from all rooms and levels. I suspect that this lack is due to the absence of these birds in any significant numbers from the Hopi mesa area rather than to the attitude of the Hopis toward this bird as a food source.

The taxonomic listings of the animals from the three cultural areas under discussion are by no means presented to indicate only food preferences. The birds were undoubtedly captured for their feathers or for ceremonial use. The smaller rodents may have served as dietary supplements or more likely may have entered the site as intrusive burrowers. One tibia of a domestic dog from room 296 was made into a pointed awl, as was a tibia from a jackrabbit.

The rooms from this area of Awatovi were abandoned long before the first Spanish settlers moved onto Antelope Mesa and, as anticipated, no introduced animals were identified from the material that was examined.

HOPI DWELLING UNITS
NORTH OF CHURCH II

Pueblo IV to Early Pueblo V, A. D. 1300 - 1700, fauna from rooms 500, 508, 516, 520, 600, 604, 606, 607, 608, 609, 610, 611, 613, 614, 615, 616, 619, 620, 622, 623, 624, and 625.

Taxonomic List

Indigenous Animals	Percentage
Lepus californicus, Black-tailed Jackrabbit	20.0
Sylvilagus auduboni, Desert Cottontail	14.0
Cynomys gunnisoni, White-tailed Prairie Dog	2.5
Citellus variegatus, Rock Squirrel	.9
Castor canadensis, Beaver	1.2
Neotoma albigula, White-throated Wood Rat	.3
Erethizon dorsatum, Porcupine	1.5
Canis familiaris, Domestic Dog	3.4
Taxidea taxus, Badger	1.2
Lynx rufus, Bobcat	2.5
Odocoileus hemionus, Mule Deer	12.5
Antilocapra americana, Pronghorned Antelope	7.5
Ovis canadensis, Desert Bighorn Sheep	.9
Buteo regalis, Ferruginous Hawk	.3
Buteo jamaicensis, Red-tailed Hawk	.9
Buteo swainsoni, Swainson's Hawk	.3
Aquila chrysaetos, Golden Eagle	.6
Falco mexicanus, Prairie Falcon	.3
Bubo virginianus, Great Horned Owl	.6
Corvus corax, Raven	2.1
Chrysemys picta, Western Painted Turtle	.3
Introduced Animals	
Equus caballus, Domestic Horse	1.5
Sus scrofa, Domestic Pig	2.8
Bos taurus, Domestic Cow	3.7
Ovis/Capra, Domestic Sheep/Goat	16.8
Gallus gallus, Domestic Chicken	.6
Total	99.2

It appears that the two occupation units immediately to the north of Spanish Church II would be the likely area that housed those Hopis who were cooperating with Franciscans. Ceramics, however, indicate that at least some rooms were occupied as early as A. D. 1300 while others may have been occupied through the Hopi rebellion and until the abandonment of Awatovi in A. D. 1701.

As with the prehistoric occupation of Antelope Mesa, heavy reliance was placed on the jackrabbits and cottontails as a basic food supply but supplemented by a sizable percentage of sheep and goats with an occasional cow and pig. The horse bones also had evidence of butchering on the condyles and may have added a change of diet. I must add that a bit of horse interjected into one's everyday food supply, which in reality does not vary to any great extent, can at times be quite pleasant. I recall the number of times that I ordered and ate with great pleasure the horse steaks that were a specialty of the Harvard Faculty Club. This meat was preferred by many of the diners over the generally chosen beef steaks or lamb.

Many of the animals from the rooms in these units evidenced butcher cuts and hack marks, and a considerable number of the bones were burned or charred. This charring could have resulted from broiling but may also have been due to the fact that scraps were thrown into a fire to dispose of them. Several sheep lumbar vertebrae were sawed along the long axis of the centrum to "halve" them; so at least some Spanish butchering tools were utilized. Whether this was done in the church kitchen or in the Hopi dwellings cannot be proven from the skeletal evidence. A number of sheep/goat hyoids were also recovered. As these bones usually stay with the tongue when the animal is butchered, it is likely that the pueblo dwellers enjoyed an occasional feast of sheep tongue. A fragment of turtle plastron from room 620 was not associated with a burial. Whether it was residue from a meal or was a portion of a leg rattle cannot be stated because identifying evidence for either case is lacking.

The largest and oldest pig (fig. 12) was from the zero - 50 cm level of room 623. Its presence in this portion of the settlement is not explained. One associated lamb skeleton was also recovered from this same level of room 623. No evidence of butchering or burning was present on the bones.

POSTREBELLION HOPI ADDITIONS TO CHURCH II

Pueblo Revolt, A. D. 1680 - 1692, fauna from rooms 483, 724, 737, 738, and 754.

Taxonomic List

Indigenous Animals	Percentage
Lepus californicus, Black-tailed Jackrabbit	16.6
Sylvilagus auduboni, Desert Cottontail	11.1
Thomomys bottae, Valley Pocket Gopher	5.5
Odocoileus hemionus, Mule Deer	11.1
Antilocapra americana, Pronghorned Antelope	5.5
Introduced Animals	
Sus scrofa, Domestic Pig	5.5
Ovis/Capra, Domestic Sheep/Goat	38.8
Gallus gallus, Domestic Chicken	5.5
Total	99.6

The rooms listed above were those constructed by the Hopis within the Spanish structure of Church II after the Pueblo Revolt of 1680 (fig. 18). They were, at least in part, occupied by the Hopis until the return of the Franciscans soon after 1692. Not all of the rooms were habitation areas. Some were stock pens or storage areas. Several bore evidence that they had been used as sheep corrals for a considerable time as layers of sheep manure had accumulated in some to a considerable depth (Montgomery, Smith, and Brew 1949).

A rather substantial reliance was still placed on jackrabbits and cottontails, probably because the inhabitants preferred this food source, but a noticeable increase is noted in the utilization of sheep/goat, once they were under complete control of the Indians. Deer and antelope continued to be a significant addition to the menu.

Comparing the change in food selection from the prehistoric Western Mound, through the Spanish occupation to the return to an Indian-dominated society, one can see at least a few significant differences.

The earliest dwellers at Awatovi relied heavily on the rabbits (62 percent of all food), supplemented by deer and antelope. When the Spanish arrived, bringing their livestock, the Hopis still hunted and ate rabbits (34 percent of all food), supplemented by deer and antelope. However, they obtained, with Franciscan permission, a 17 percent addition of sheep/goat to their diet with small amounts of pig, cow, and horse. Once the Hopis had complete charge of the domestic animals abandoned by the Franciscans in 1680, the diet changed again. Rabbits constituted only 28 percent of the food but were still augmented by deer and antelope. However, the use of sheep/goat jumped to 39 percent of all food used. The sample examined for this period showed pig still being used but no cows or horses.

This lack of cows and horses in the tabulations is probably due to some degree to sample selection rather than to the conditions that actually existed from 1680 to 1692. In both of the latter cultural areas the domestic chickens played only a small part in the food preferences of the Hopis. This may be due to the simple fact that the inhabitants never acquired a taste for fowl. After all the turkey was never a very important part of the pre-Hispanic Awatovian's diet.

EVIDENCE OF BUTCHERING

In principle I agree with the oft-repeated statement that in many areas and among a wide variety of peoples there are butchering practices that follow cultural patterns. I do, however, disagree that one can always interpret the evidence of butchering that is present on excavated bones as representing a certain culture. This is particularly true at Awatovi in those areas where there is a mixture of Spanish and Hopi residue plus additions from cultures not known.

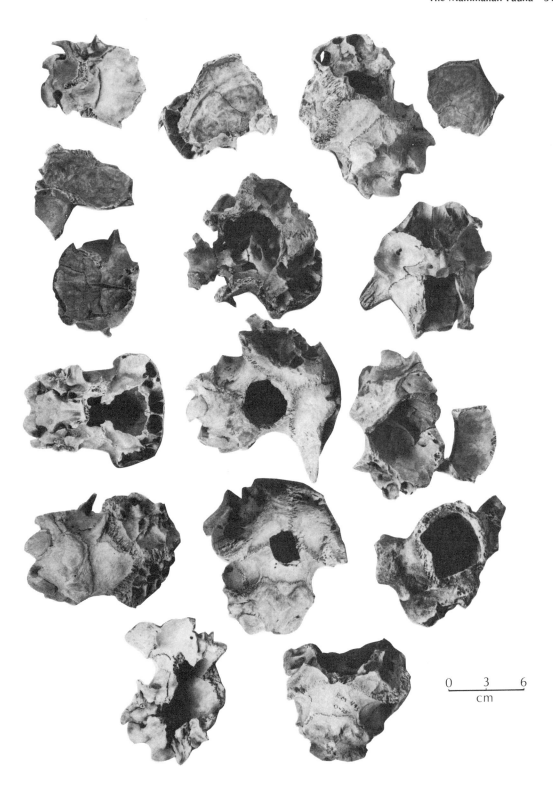

Figure 19.   Crania of domestic sheep and goats from Awatovi, broken for removal of brains.

Figure 20.   A, contents of a single vessel from the southeast corner of room 6, test 24 at Awatovi, one individual of a desert cottontail is represented; B, accumulation of burned and charred domestic sheep bones from a fire pit in a Hopi dwelling.

For example, we have no knowledge of who butchered for the Franciscan kitchen and if he were Spanish or Indian. If it were a Franciscan, where was the geographic area where he initially obtained his butchering skills? It would be just as likely that he learned on the job as did many priests when they were confronted with the numerous tasks of church carpentry and masonry in building the missions of the Southwest. If the butchers were Indian, were they in reality tutored in these crafts, or did they butcher to their own individual tastes or under the guidance of European priests? Observance of the many hacking cuts and false starts on the various bones of sheep indicate a low level of skill at disarticulating the skeletons of an animal (fig. 16).

How does one differentiate between cut marks on bone that were made when the animals were first cut up as opposed to cut marks made on cooked bones to separate articulated joints at a non-table meal? I have yet to find a way to distinguish between the cuts left on a bone from removing the hide as compared to separating the same joints for culinary purposes — agreeing of course that not all Awatovi meat cutters were trained butchers with a surgeon's touch.

It is also possible for a well-trained butcher to skin and separate a carcass without leaving any marks on the bones. This would go unrecorded and perhaps such an animal would not be regarded as part of the food source.

The foregoing is mentioned only to support the hypothesis that very little, that is not supposition, can be stated as to cultural butchering techniques when such statements are based on as many outside influences as were present at Awatovi.

The numerous sawed and hacked horn cores and horn-core bases of the skulls of both sheep and goats (fig. 16) may have been the result of the removal of these elements so that the skulls would fit into cooking vessels. Tongue, eyes, and the meat adhering to the heads of these animals would have been acceptable food. A great number of sheep and goats (fig. 19), as well as antelope, had the crania broken for the removal of the brain, presumably for food. However, one must also consider the possible use of brains along with woodashes and other ingredients for the purpose of tanning hides. This method of processing buckskin is still in use in some areas of the Southwest. The great majority of bones of all species of food animals were cracked and broken. Few were entire. This was probably done to obtain the marrow from the inside of the bones. It added many hours to the task of determining what animals were present at Awatovi and in what proportions.

OCCURRENCES OF ANIMALS IN KIVAS AND VESSELS

Kiva A, situated about 22 meters west of room 528 and about 72 meters northeast of test 14, was originally constructed sometime in the early fifteenth century (Smith 1972). On the bench of the Kiva next to a loom weight was the complete skeleton of a domestic sheep (ibid., p. 45, fig. 27). This skeleton was not collected entire, and only a partial skull could be identified as belonging to this individual. Other remains of sheep were found in Kiva I of test 22. Burned vertebrae and ribs represented this animal in Kiva I. Kiva II produced a few metapodials. Deer bones were found in Kiva I, II, and VII. Remains of domestic cow and dog and of cottontail rabbit were also recovered from the floor of Kiva VII and the Kiva fill of room 844. Bones of the turkey were present on the floor of Kiva I and in Kivas II and VII. Breast and tail feathers of turkeys are used on Kachina masks and prayer sticks (Smith and Ewing 1952); so their presence in the Kivas is expected. The remains of an eagle were found in the fill of Kiva VII and a red-tailed hawk on the floor of Kiva II. These are also birds that would be logical additions to the Kiva fauna. Many of the bones had cut marks indicating separating the various bones at the joints. This would be a logical procedure if the wings of the birds were disjointed from the bodies in order to obtain the large wing feathers.

Several accumulations of mammal bones in pottery vessels were collected. One such occurrence was found in a bowl located in the southeast corner of room 6 of test 14. They represented a good deal of the skeleton of a single desert cottontail (fig. 20, A).

Several deposits of burned and charred sheep bones were concentrated in fire pits. The broken and burned bones in fire pit A (fig. 20, B) were found in the floor of room 13.

After many months of sorting, identifying, and analyzing all of the 37,000 bone fragments from Awatovi, it is apparent that excavation of the remaining 90 percent of the site will answer many questions that arose out of this initial study. Undoubtedly, many new and interesting additions to our knowledge of the early use of the animals by the inhabitants of Awatovi will also result from a continuation of excavations on Antelope Mesa.

References

Boessneck, J., H.H. Müller, and M. Teichert
  1964 *Osteologische Unterscheidungsmerkmale zwischen Schaf* (Ovis aries *Linné) und Ziege (*Capra hircus *Linné). Kuhn-Archiv, Akademie-Verlag, Berlin, 129 pp.

Bradfield, M.
  1974 *Birds of The Hopi Region, Their Names, and Notes on Their Ecology.* Bulletin no. 48, Museum of Northern Arizona, Flagstaff, 75 pp.

Briggs, H.M.
  1970 *Modern Breeds of Livestock.* The Macmillan Co., New York, 714 pp.

Buechner, H.K.
  1960 *The Bighorn Sheep in the United States, Its Past, Present and Future.* Wildlife Society, Monograph no. 4, Chestertown, Maryland, 174 pp.

Cockrum, E.L.
  1960 *The Recent Mammals of Arizona.* The University of Arizona Press, Tucson, 276 pp.

Hall, E.R., and K.R. Kelson
  1959 *The Mammals of North America* (2 vols). The Ronald Press Co., New York, 1083 pp.

Hargrave, L.L.
  1939 "Bird Bones from Abandoned Indian Dwellings in Arizona and Utah," *The Condor,* vol. 41, pp. 206-210, Berkeley.

Lawrence, B.
  1951 *Mammals Found at the Awatovi Site.* Papers of the Peabody Museum, Harvard University, vol. 35, no. 3, part 1, pp. 3-4, Cambridge, Massachusetts.

Montgomery, R.G., W. Smith, and J.O. Brew
  1949 *Franciscan Awatovi.* Papers of the Peabody Museum, Harvard University, vol. 36, Cambridge, Massachusetts, 361 pp.

Smith, Watson
  1972 *Prehistoric Kivas of Antelope Mesa.* Papers of the Peabody Museum, Harvard University, vol. 39, no. 1, Cambridge, Massachusetts, 162 pp.

Smith, Watson, and L. Ewing
  1952 *Kiva Mural Decorations at Awatovi and Kawai Ka-a.* Papers of the Peabody Museum, Harvard University, vol. 37, Cambridge, Massachusetts, 363 pp.

Smith, Watson, R.B. Woodbury, and N.F.S. Woodbury
  1966 *The Excavation of Hawikuh By Frederick Webb Hodge.* Contributions from the Museum of the American Indian, Heye Foundation, vol. 20, New York, 336 pp.

Underhill, R.
  1956 *The Navajos.* University of Oklahoma Press, Norman, 288 pp.

White, T.E.
  1953 "A Method of Calculating the Dietary Percentage of Various Food Animals Utilized By Aboriginal Peoples," *American Antiquity,* vol. 18, no. 4, April, pp. 396-398, Salt Lake City.

Woodbury, A.M., and H.N. Russell
  1945 *Birds of the Navajo Country.* Bulletin of the University of Utah, vol. 35, no. 14, Salt Lake City, 157 pp.

Number 2

BONE AND ANTLER ARTIFACTS

Richard Page Wheeler

Contents

Figures

Preface

The artifacts described in this paper were recovered in the course of archaeological investigations that were conducted by the Peabody Museum Awatovi Expedition, under the direction of Dr. J.O. Brew, during five seasons, 1935-1939, at Awatovi and nearby sites in the Hopi Indian Reservation in northeastern Arizona. In early 1936, I began a study of the stone and bone artifacts returned to Cambridge from the 1935 excavations, and in the 1936 and 1937 seasons I spent my entire time, with the help of two able assistants, Marion Hutchinson Tschopik and Dorothy Newton, cataloguing stone, bone, and antler artifacts in the field. In the 1938 and 1939 seasons, Richard Woodbury replaced me as field cataloguer of these categories of artifacts (aided by three or four members of the Expedition staff), and he carried out a number of small archaeological excavations as well. Using records and notes compiled by both of us for the more than 8,000 stone artifacts obtained during the five seasons of fieldwork, Dr. Woodbury published in 1954 a 240-page monograph entitled *Prehistoric Stone Implements of Northeastern Arizona*.

Sometime in 1964, while I was serving as laboratory supervisor of the Wetherill Mesa Project at Mesa Verde National Park, I mentioned in a conversation with Dr. Brew, Chairman of the Project's Advisory Committee, that, in addition to running the Wetherill laboratory, I was preparing reports on the stone and bone artifacts from Long House, one of the major sites excavated and stabilized by the Project at Wetherill Mesa. I asked Dr. Brew about the status of the bone and antler artifacts accumulated by the Peabody Museum Awatovi Expedition and was amazed to learn that they had never been touched. Would he consider giving me a crack at them at long last? "Why not?" was his quick reply. And it was not long afterward that two specially built wooden packing cases containing the material, heavily insured, arrived at Mesa Verde. Regrettably, I was so hard pressed to wind up the Project's records by a fixed date, June 25, 1965, that my examination of the Arizona material barely got under way before it was time to wrap it up and ship it back to Massachusetts.

But for people like Dr. Woodbury and Dr. Brew, most logistical problems are of little importance. In the autumn of 1965, Dr. Woodbury was head of the Department of Anthropology at the Smithsonian, and I was ensconced in Washington as an editor with the Division of Archeology of the National Park Service. After Dr. Woodbury had found a spare room for me to work in at the Museum of Natural History building and had obtained a guest pass for me, Dr. Brew shipped the two superb wooden packing cases of bone and antler artifacts to Washington. I finished analyzing the material, and picked out specimens for illustration, during weekends over a three-months' period in 1965-1966.

Once the material was back at the Peabody Museum, Dr. Brew had the selected specimens photographed, and he arranged with Barbara Lawrence of the Museum of Comparative Zoology to make as complete faunal identifications of the artifacts as possible. In October 1967, I visited the Brews and consulted with Barbara Lawrence in Cambridge, and I borrowed thirty-odd bone artifacts, mostly of bird bone. These were identified for me by Charmion R. McKusick, formerly a member of the staff of the Southwestern (now Western) Archeological Center, National Park Service, and now operating the Southwest Bird Lab, affiliated with the Amerind Foundation, and by Professor Stanley J. Olsen, Department of Anthropology, the University of Arizona.

I am very grateful to everyone named above (and unnamed) who contributed to this study, especially Dr. Brew, esteemed friend and mentor for over four decades, and I want to express warm thanks to Dr. Stephen Williams, former director of the Peabody Museum, and his staff, for encouragement and for supplying provenience data missing from my notes; to Watson Smith, stout friend of old and more recent Awatovi days, for moral support; and to Greta Crais, kind friend and neighbor, for converting puzzling handwriting into pellucid typescript.

In assigning chronological placements to most of the artifacts dealt with in this paper, I have followed Richard Woodbury's scheme for the stone artifacts from the same district. This was based on ceramic typology, using the original Pecos Classification (Woodbury 1954, pp. 5-15).

R.P.W.

Alexandria, Virginia

Artifacts of Bone

Bones used by the people of Awatovi and neighboring villages for artifacts were the by-products of hunting or snaring, or of the butchering of both the aboriginally domesticated dog and turkey and of the Spanish-introduced horse or mule, cattle, sheep and/or goats, and possibly greyhound (Olsen 1976). As will be shown, bone material, unlike stone, was rather easily fabricated into a variety of functional and aesthetic forms. The ready accessibility of bone and the comparative ease with which it could be worked may explain the dispersal of still serviceable bone artifacts — lost? misplaced? — throughout the sites. Here, as elsewhere, many fragile bone artifacts carried a high degree of "use polish" that seems to have aided in their preservation.

For convenience of description, the bone artifacts from the Jeddito District have been grouped as follows:

Classification and Tabulation

Tools   1,011

Awls   846

Style M(Mammal)1:   long bones, also splint bones; whole shaft pared and ground to point, joint intact   143

Style M1a: long bone; whole shaft (joined left radius-ulna) pared and ground to point, joint intact   1

Style M1b: long bone; whole shaft pared and ground to point, then incised, joint carved and inlaid   1

Style M2:   long bones; whole shaft pared and ground to point at one end, pared and ground or roughly broken at other end   97

Style M3:   long bones longitudinally severed through shaft and joint; shaft pared and ground to point, joint unmodified or only slightly modified   28

Style M4:   long bones longitudinally severed through shaft and joint; shaft pared and ground to point, joint greatly modified by grinding and polishing   82

Style M5:   long bone splinters; one end pared and ground to point, other end (butt) irregular or rounded by cutting and grinding   432

Style M5a: long bone splinters; each end pared and ground to point   5

Style M6:   ribs; whole or longitudinally split section pared and ground to point at one end, unmodified or cut and ground at other end   4

Style B(Bird)1:   long bones; whole shaft pared and ground to point, proximal joint intact   7

Style B2:   long bones; whole shaft pared and ground to point, distal joint intact   4

Style B3:   long bones; whole shaft pared and ground to point, joint cut off or broken off   5

Style B4:   long bones; whole shaft, medial section, one end sliced obliquely and ground to point, other end cut and ground or broken off   3

Style B5:   long bone splinters; one end pared and ground to point, other end (usually) broken off irregularly   11

Style M or B: long bone splinters; one end pared and ground to point, other end usually cut and broken off   23

Awl spatulas   15
Bodkins   2
Punches   30
Needles   38
Pins   9
Spatulas   14
End scrapers   33
Miscellaneous utility   23

Musical Instruments   21
Sounding-rasps   17
Whistles   4

Ornaments   526
Tubular beads — individual   204
Tubular and flat rectangular beads — in 8 clusters   287
Pendants or beads — individual   28
Pendants or beads — in 1 cluster   7

Other Artifacts   90
Gaming pieces or dice   20
Stock   70
Total: **1,647**

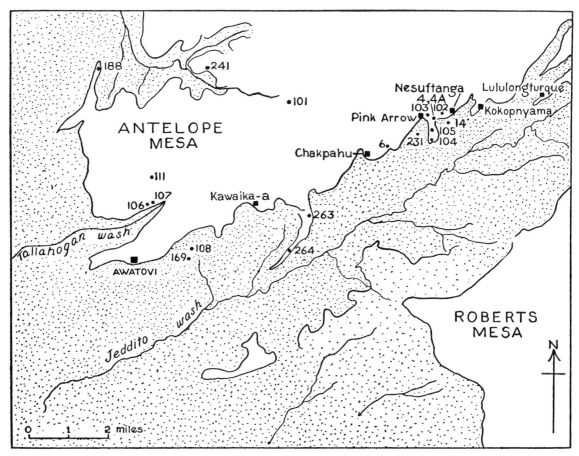

Figure 1. Archaeological sites recorded in the Jeddito District. The sites underlined yielded material dealt with in this paper. (Source: Woodbury 1954, fig. 2, p. 7.)

TOOLS

Awls

By far the most numerous bone tools in this collection, as in every such collection of which I am aware, are awls, made from mammal or bird bones (usually long bones), or from elements so altered in joint and shaft that they cannot be identified as either mammal or bird. Bone awls are perforating implements, generally single pointed, which vary from tiny, neatly fashioned instruments to rather large robust ones, and include some of the most fortuitous slivers imaginable. Presumably, they were used to pierce hides and other tough fabrics, and also to make baskets. Whole specimens taper to a point with a fine tip that is frequently polished by use.

MAMMAL BONE AWLS

Seven hundred and ninety-three complete or fragmentary awls from Awatovi and nearby sites were made from mammal bones. All but five of them are single pointed. Six principal styles are recognized.

Style M1: Long bones, also splint bones; the proximal or distal end of the whole shaft is pared (that is, removed as if by chipping, shaving, or whittling away) and ground to a short or long, tapered, symmetrical or asymmetrical point, and the joint is unmodified, supposedly for use as a handle or grip. The 101 complete and 42 fragmentary awls of this style are tabulated according to species and elements on page 45.

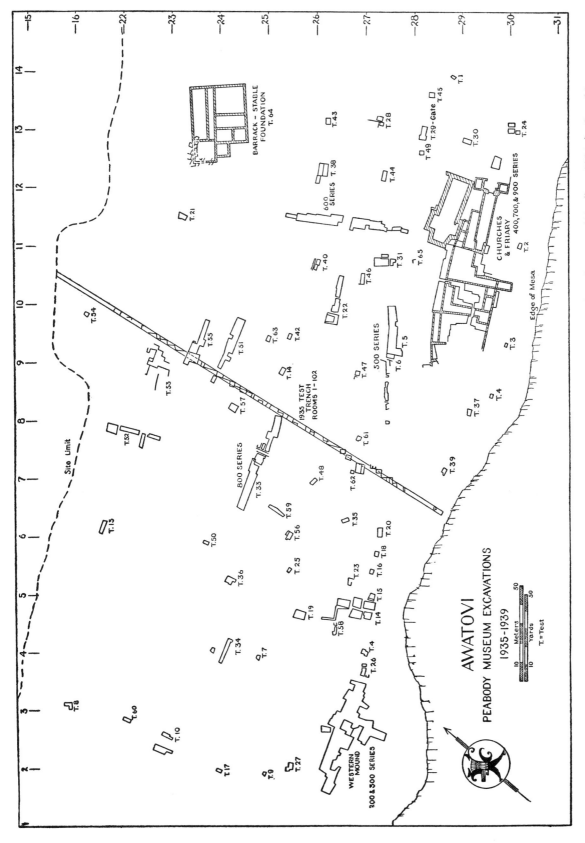

Figure 2. Awatovi, showing locations of excavations, 1935–1939. Individual rooms are not indicated. (Source: Woodbury 1954, fig. 3, p. 8.)

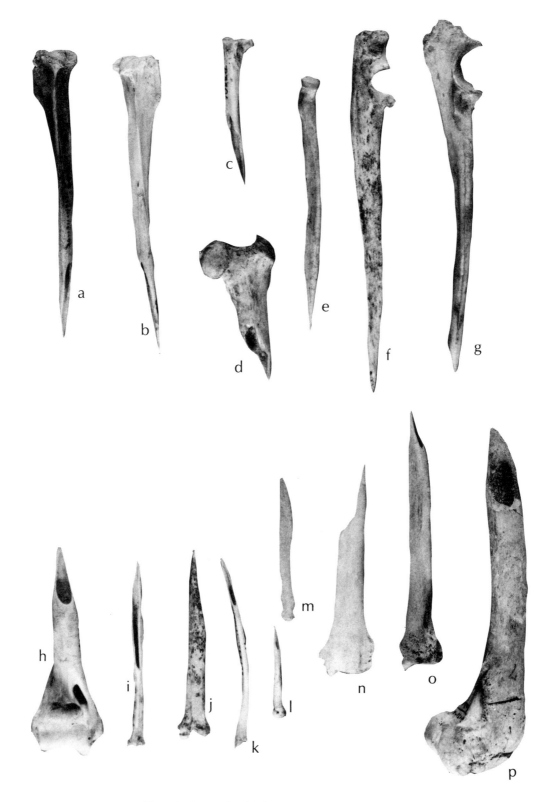

Figure 3. Bone awls of Style M1. Length of p is 13.6 cm.

Figure	Species	Element	Count
3a	*Lepus californicus,* black-tailed jackrabbit	right tibia, proximal end	15
		right tibia, distal end	6
3b		left tibia, proximal	17
		left tibia, distal	2
		right radius, proximal	1
		left radius, distal	1
		right ulna, proximal	1
		left ulna, proximal	3
3c	*Lynx rufus,* bobcat	metatarsal	1
3d		left femur, proximal	1
3e		left radius, proximal	1
		right radius, distal	2
		left radius, distal	5
3f		right ulna, proximal	7
		left ulna, proximal	7
3g	*Canis* cf. *familiaris,* domestic dog	left radius, proximal	1
		right radius, distal	1
		right ulna, proximal	4
	Canis sp. dog or coyote	right ulna, proximal	10
		left ulna, proximal	3
		left humerus, proximal	1
		left fused tibia-fibula, distal	1
3h	*Lynx rufus,* bobcat	right humerus, distal	1
3i	*Sylvilagus auduboni,* desert cottontail	left femur, distal	1
		right tibia, proximal	3
		left tibia, proximal	4
3j	*Lepus californicus,* black-tailed jackrabbit	right femur, distal	1
3k		left radius, proximal	6
		right radius, proximal	2
3l		metapodial	1
		left femur, proximal	1
3m	*Odocoileus hemionus,* mule deer	left splint	1
		right splint	1
3n	*Canis* cf. *familiaris,* domestic dog	left radius, distal	2
3o	*Canis* cf. *latrans,* coyote	right radius, distal	1
		right ulna, proximal	8
		left humerus, distal	1
3p	*Canis* cf. *familiaris,* domestic dog	left femur, distal	1
	Ovis canadensis, bighorn sheep	metatarsal, distal	1
	Taxidea taxus, badger	left ulna, proximal	1
4, *left*	Artiodactyl	femur, distal	1
		left ulna, proximal	2
	?	right ulna, proximal	3
	?	left ulna, proximal	8
	?	right splint	1
		Total	143

Figure 4. Bone awls of Style M1, left, and M1a, right. Length of M1a is 16.4 cm.

Measurements: The complete awls of Style M1 (101 specimens) range in overall length from 5 to 15 cm, and the tapered points of these awls range from 0.3 to 10 cm in length. The tips of these points are needle sharp in 70 cases and are rounded and "flaked back" in 16 and 15 cases, respectively. Eighty-four awls of Style M1 having intact points show use polish and 17 have what might be termed a satiny finish.

Provenience:

Site 4A, Basket Maker III - early Pueblo I	1
Site 264, Basket Maker III - early Pueblo I	1
Site 111, early Pueblo II	1
Site 169, early Pueblo II	1
Site 102, Pueblo II	1
Site 105, Pueblo II - Pueblo III	1
Pink Arrow, Pueblo III - IV	4
Awatovi, Pueblo III - V	131
Unassigned	2
Total	143

Style M1a: Long bone; the whole shaft — the distal end of a fused left radius-ulna of *Odocoileus hemionus,* mule deer — is pared and ground to a short, tapered asymmetrical point, and the joint is unmodified, probably for use as a handle or grip. Measuring 16.4 cm in overall length, this awl is slightly blunted at the tip by flaking back and shows a rather high degree of use polish (fig. 4, *right*).
Provenience:
Awatovi, Pueblo IV - V

Style M1b: Long bone; the whole shaft — the distal end of a metatarsal of *Odocoileus hemionus,* mule deer — is pared and ground to a short, tapered, slightly asymmetrical point, and the joint (butt) is carved, ground, and inlaid. At the top is what appears to be a dog (?) effigy, with a "head" consisting of carved ears and muzzle, an incised mouth, and a pair of inlaid green-blue turquoise eyes, one trapezoidal and one oblong, each 2 mm in maximum diameter; and a carved arched "tail" opposite the "head." Under the effigy is a straight-through, flat oval perforation, 1.9 cm across and 0.75 cm high; and below the perforation, at the top of the cylindrical shaft itself, is an encircling band of incised crisscross lines forming small squares, 1.7 cm wide (fig. 5).

Figure 5. Bone awl of Style M1b. Length is 11.8 cm.

This awl, the only one of the sort found in the Jeddito District, has these overall dimensions: length, 11.8 cm; width, 3.2 cm; thickness, 1.9 cm. The point is 3 cm in length. The tip is slightly rounded and highly polished from use.

Provenience:

Site 111, early Pueblo II

Seemingly, effigy awls were a rarity everywhere in the prehistoric Southwest for I have run across only two other examples reported in the literature, both recovered at Hawikuh, near Zuni, New Mexico. In one case, Hodge described a carved awl handle (butt) as representing a mountain sheep; in the other, the carved awl represented a Shumaikoli mask, according to Hodge's Zuni workmen (Hodge 1920, fig. 20, p. 93, and fig. 21, p 94).

Style M2: Long bones; the whole shaft is pared and ground to a short or long, tapered, symmetrical or asymmetrical point at one end and is pared and ground or roughly broken at the other end. The 55 complete and 42 fragmentary awls of this style are tabulated by species and elements as follows:

Figure 6. Bone awls of Style M2. Length of awl at left is 12 cm.

Figure	Species	Element	Count
	Lepus californicus, black-tailed jackrabbit	radius, left or right (?)	7
		left radius	1
		right radius, distal end	1
		tibia, left or right (?)	5
		right tibia	3
		right tibia, proximal end	1
		left tibia, proximal	5
		right ulna, proximal	1
		right femur, proximal	2
	Lynx rufus, bobcat	right tibia, proximal	3
		tibia, proximal	1
		right ulna, proximal	3
		left ulna , proximal	1
	Felis sp.	radius	1
		right ulna, proximal	1
	Carnivore (?)	radius	7
		ulna, distal	1
		left ulna, proximal	1
		tibia, distal	3
		right tibia, proximal	1
		left tibia, proximal	1
	Canis sp. dog or coyote	left tibia, proximal	2
		radius	2
		humerus	1
		right humerus, proximal	3
6, *left*		right ulna, proximal	3

		left ulna, proximal	4
		right ulna, proximal	1
		left ulna, proximal	2
	Sylvilagus auduboni, desert cottontail	left tibia, proximal	1
	Artiodactyl	radius	1
		left ulna , proximal	1
		right ulna, proximal	1
		right ulna, distal	2
		metatarsal	1
6, *right*	Unidentifiable		22
		Total	97

Measurements: The 55 intact awls of Style M2 range in overall length from 4.8 to 13.4 cm, and the tapered points of these awls range from 1.1 to 6.5 cm in length. The tips of these points are needle sharp in 26 cases, rounded in 23 cases, and flaked back in 6 cases. Twenty-nine of the complete awls show use polish and 7 have a satiny finish near the tip.

Provenience:

Site 264, Basket Maker III - Pueblo I	1
Site 107, Pueblo I - Pueblo III	1
Site 103, Pueblo II	1
Pink Arrow, Pueblo III - IV	8
Awatovi, Pueblo III - V	86
Total	97

Style M3: Long bones longitudinally severed through shaft and joint; shaft pared and ground to short or long, tapered, symmetrical point; joint unmodified or only slightly modified by cutting and grinding, and used as a handle or grip. The 23 complete and 5 fragmentary awls of this style are listed by species and elements below.

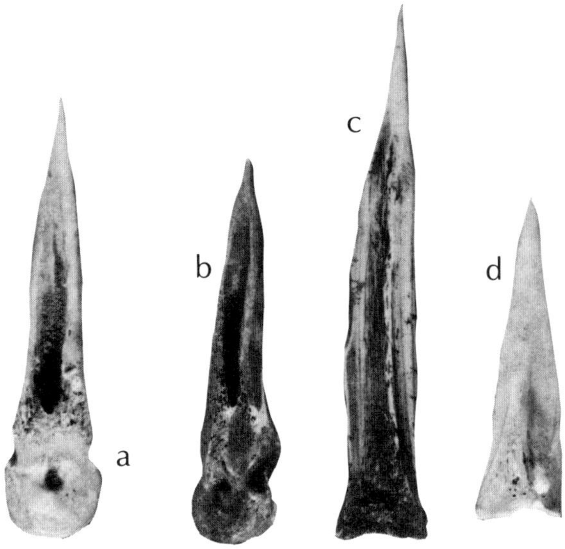

Figure 7. Bone awls of Style M3. Length of c is 11 cm.

Figure	Species	Element	Count
	Antilocapra americana, pronghorn	metatarsal, proximal end	2
7a		metatarsal, distal end	1
7b		metacarpal, distal	4
	Odocoileus hemionus, mule deer	tibia, distal	1
		metatarsal, proximal	6
		metatarsal, distal	2
		metacarpal, proximal	1
		metacarpal, distal	2
	Artiodactyl	radius, proximal	1
		tibia, distal	1
7c		metatarsal, proximal	1
7d		metapodial, proximal	2
	probably Artiodactyl	metapodial	3
	Unidentifiable		1
		Total	28

Measurements: The 23 complete awls of Style M3 range in overall length from 4 to 24.9 cm, and their tapered points range from 0.8 to 4.5 cm in length. The tips of these points are sharp in 5 cases, rounded in 13 cases, and flaked back in 6 instances. Seventeen of the intact awls show use polish near the tip.

Provenience:

Site 264, Basket Maker III - Pueblo I	2
Pink Arrow, Pueblo III - IV	3
Awatovi, Pueblo III - V	22
Unassigned	1
Total	28

Style M4: Long bones longitudinally severed through shaft and joint; shaft pared and ground to short or long, tapered symmetrical point; joint greatly modified by grinding and polishing. The 61 complete and 21 fragmentary awls of this style are tabulated by species and elements below.

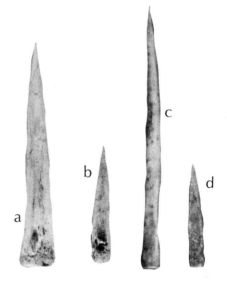

Figure 8. Bone awls of Style M4. Length of c is 12.9 cm.

Figure	Species	Element	Count
	Odocoileus hemionus, mule deer	metatarsal	8
		metatarsal, proximal end	3
8a		metacarpal, proximal	1
		metapodial	10
	Lynx rufus, bobcat	tibia, distal end	1
	Antilocapra americana, pronghorn (?)	metatarsal, proximal	1
		metacarpal, proximal	1
	Artiodactyl	metatarsal	6
		metacarpal	1
		?	6
	(?)	tibia	1
8b, 8c, 8d	Unidentifiable		43
		Total	82

Measurements: The 61 intact awls of Style M4 range in overall length from 3.7 to 21.7 cm, and the tapered points range from 1.1 to 6 cm in length. The tips of these points are sharp in 16 cases, rounded in 26 instances, and flaked back in 13 cases. Thirty-eight of the complete awls show use polish and 6 have a satiny finish near the tip.

One awl of Style M4, a rather amorphous specimen, 8.4 cm in overall length, with a point of 4.5 cm long, the tip of which is rounded by use, has six irregularly spaced grooves in the point — two in one side, two in the opposite side, and two in one face. These grooves are very short and extremely shallow, unlike the deeply notched grooves found on three awls at Aztec Ruin, New Mexico, which Morris suggested may have been produced by "drawing a cord between the implement and the thumb or finger" in order to straighten cords or thongs (Morris 1919, p. 39 and fig. 23b). The present example likewise appears to have resulted from use rather than intention.

Provenience:

Site 264, Basket Maker III - Pueblo I	1
Site 4 (Late Unit), Pueblo III	1
Pink Arrow, Pueblo III - Pueblo IV	14
Kawaika-a, Pueblo III - IV	2
Awatovi, Pueblo III - V	64
Total	82

Style M5: Long bone splinters; one end pared and ground to a short or long, tapered, symmetrical or asymmetrical point; the other end (butt) is irregular and rough, or may be rounded by cutting and grinding. The 432 awls of this style are tabulated according to species and elements as follows:

Figure	Species	Element	Count
	Odocoileus hemionus, mule deer	metatarsal	2
	Antilocapra americana, pronghorn	tibia	1
		metatarsal	1
	Felis sp.	radius	1
	Artiodactyl	femur	2
		metatarsal	1
9d		metapodial	9
	probably Artiodactyl	metapodial	6
	Artiodactyl?	metapodial?	1
	Artiodactyl?	tibia?	4
9a, 9b, 9c, 9e	Unidentifiable		404
		Total	432

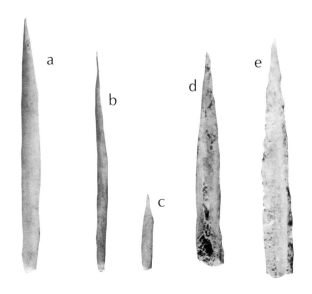

Figure 9. Bone awls of Style M5. Length of a is 9.9 cm.

Measurements: The 279 complete awls of Style M5 range in overall length from 3 to 21.2 cm, and their tapered points range from 1 to 10.5 cm in length. The tips of these awls are needle sharp in 31 cases, rounded in 168 cases, and flaked back in 68 instances. Four of these awls show a high degree of use polish and one has a satiny finish at the tip.

Provenience:

Site 4A, Basket Maker III - early Pueblo I	3
Site 264, Basket Maker III - early Pueblo I	3
Site 105, Pueblo II - III	1
Site 4 (Late Unit), Pueblo III	5

Pink Arrow, Pueblo III - IV	11
Kawaika-a, Pueblo III - IV	8
Awatovi, Pueblo III - V	387
Unassigned	13
No provenience given	1
Total	432

Style M5a: Long bone splinters; each end pared and ground to a long, tapered, symmetrical or asymmetrical point. The five awls of this style are made from long bone splinters of unidentifiable species of mammals. Four of them are complete and range in overall length from 4.8 to 8.1 cm, and their tips vary from needle sharp to slightly rounded from use (fig. 10). The fifth awl, somewhat over 8.4 cm in overall length and showing high use polish, was splintered in the course of use from the center of one tip halfway down one tapering side.

Provenience:

Awatovi, Pueblo IV - V

Style M6: Ribs; whole or longitudinally split section pared and ground to a short or long, tapered, symmetrical or asymmetrical point at one end and unmodified or cut and ground at the other end. Of the four awls of Style M6, one is made from the rib of Artiodactyl (fig. 11, *left*) but the other three are from ribs of unidentifiable mammals. They range in overall length from 5.4 to 10.8 cm, and their points range from 1 to 3.3 cm in length. In one case, the tip is sharp; in two cases, the tip is rounded; and in the fourth instance, the tip is flaked back.

Provenience:

Awatovi, Pueblo III -V	3
Unassigned	1
Total	4

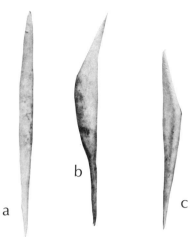

Figure 10. Bone awls of Style M5a. Length of a is 8.1 cm.

Figure 11. Bone awls of Style M6. Length of awl at left is 8.7 cm.

BIRD BONE AWLS

Thirty complete or fragmentary awls from Awatovi and nearby sites were made from bird bones. All of them are single pointed. Five styles are recognized.

Style B1: Long bones; whole shaft pared and ground to a short or long, tapered, symmetrical or asymmetrical point, and the proximal joint is unmodified, supposedly for use as a handle or grip. The three intact and four fragmentary awls of this style are listed by species and elements below.

Measurements: The three complete awls of Style B1 range in overall length from 5.7 to 11.9 cm, and their points range from 2.1 to 3.9 cm in length. The tip of one point is needle sharp, those of the other two are slightly rounded from use. They all show a high degree of use polish at the tip.

Provenience:

Site 102, early Pueblo II	1
Site 4 (Late Unit), Pueblo III	1
Awatovi, Pueblo III	4
Pink Arrow, Pueblo III - IV	1
Total	7

Figure	Species	Element	Count
12a	*Meleagris gallopavo,* turkey	right radius, proximal end	2
		left radius, proximal	2
12b		right tarsometatarsus, proximal	1
	Branta canadensis, Canada goose	left radius, proximal	1
	Unidentifiable	left radius, proximal	1
		Total	7

Figure 12. Bone awls of Styles B1, a and b; B2, c-e; B4, f; and B5, g and h. Length of c is 15.8 cm.

Style B2: Long bones; whole shaft pared and ground to short or long, tapered, symmetrical or asymmetrical point, and distal joint is unmodified, or slightly ground, presumably for use as a handle or grip. The four complete awls of this style are tabulated by species and elements as follows:

Figure	Species	Element	Count
12c	*Meleagris gallopavo,* turkey	left tibiotarsus, distal end	1
12d		left tarsometatarsus, distal	1
12e		left radius, distal	1
	Branta canadensis, Canada goose	left radius, distal	1
		Total	4

Measurements: The four awls of Style B2 range in overall length from 4.9 to 15.8 cm, and their points range from 1.9 to 6.4 cm in length. The tip of one point is sharp, and the tips of the other three points are rounded.

Provenience:

Site 103, Pueblo II	1
Awatovi, Pueblo III - V	3
Total	4

Style B3: Long bones, whole shaft pared and ground to a short or long, tapered, symmetrical or asymmetrical point, and joint is cut off or broken off. The three complete and two fragmentary awls of this style are listed by species and elements below.

Measurements: The three complete awls of Style B3 range in overall length from 8.8 to 11 cm, and their points range from 1.2 to 3.6 cm in length. The tips of two of the points show high use polish and that of the third has a satiny finish.

Provenience:
   Awatovi, Pueblo III - IV

Figure	Species	Element	Count
	Meleagris gallopavo, turkey	right tibiotarsus, proximal end	2
		left tibiotarsus, distal end	2
	Buteo, sp. Buteonine hawk	left radius, proximal	1
		Total	5

Style B4: Long bones; whole shaft, medial section, one end sliced obliquely and ground to a long, tapering, symmetrical point, other end (butt) cut and ground or broken off. The single complete awl of this style is the distal end of a left tibiotarsus of *Meleagris gallopavo,* turkey. Its overall length is 11.9 cm, and its point is 4.8 cm in length. The tip is rounded (fig. 12f). The other two fragmentary awls of Style B4 are made from unidentifiable leg bones.

Provenience:
   Awatovi, Pueblo III

Style B5: Long bone splinters; one end cut and ground to a short or long, tapering, symmetrical or asymmetrical point, other end (usually) broken off irregularly. The 11 awls of this style — ten complete and one fragmentary — were made from splinters of leg bones of unidentifiable species of birds (fig. 12g and h).

Measurements: The ten complete awls of Style B5 range in length from 4.7 to 7.5 cm, and their points range from 1.3 to 3.9 cm in length. The tips of all these points bear a high use polish.

Provenience:
Site 264, Basket Maker III - Pueblo I	2
Awatovi, Pueblo III	4
Awatovi, Pueblo IV	5
Total	11

Style M/B: Bone splinters; one end pared and ground to a short or long, tapering, symmetrical or asymmetrical point, other end usually cut and broken off. The 23 awls of this style — 15 complete and 8 fragmentary — were made from long bones of unidentifiable mammals or birds.

Measurements: The 15 complete awls of Style M/B range in length from 3.9 to 12.6 cm, and their points range from 1.3 to 6.7 cm in length. Tips of these awls are generally smoothed, and in only two cases were they noticeably use polished.

Provenience:
Site 169, early Pueblo II	1
Kawaika-a, Pueblo III - IV	1
Awatovi, Pueblo III	12
Awatovi, Pueblo IV	6
Awatovi, Pueblo V	3
Total	23

Awl Spatulas

Fifteen finished, complete artifacts made from long bones of unidentifiable mammals are characterized by a long, tapering, symmetrical or asymmetrical point at one end (fig. 13a-d) — or a short, constricted (resharpened?) point at one end (fig. 13e) — and a relatively wide, beveled, and round or slightly pointed or oblique edge at the other end. The marked contrast in the two ends of these tools has given rise in the literature to the designation "awl spatulas," and this seems appropriate.

The 15 specimens range in length from 3.9 to 13.5 cm. About half of them show a high degree of use polish. It is possible that one exceptionally gracile example (fig. 13d), measuring 6.5 by 0.25 by 0.2 cm, should have been classified as an eyeless needle.

Provenience:
Site 4A, Pueblo III	1
Awatovi, Pueblo III - V	14
Total	15

Bodkins

Two bone artifacts in the collection have been classed as "bodkins," or blunt needles with large eyes. Each is finished and complete. One of them (fig. 13f), a longitudinally split, ground, and smoothed metapodial of artiodactyl, measures 14.9 by 1.6 by 0.7 cm. The sides at the distal end are pared and ground to a tapering, symmetrical point about 2.2 cm in length, with a constricted (resharpened?) tip about 0.8 cm in length. The point is use polished and the tip is blunted. A round perforation, 3 mm in diameter, started from each face, occurs 1.35 cm above the slightly convex, polished butt.

Provenience:
   Awatovi, Pueblo III

The other bodkin (fig. 13g), made from the long bone splinter of an unidentifiable mammal, measures 9.1 by 1.5 by 0.45 cm. The sides are pared and ground at one end to a long, tapering, constricted point, 1.8 cm in

length, with a needle sharp tip, and at the other end are pared and ground to a rounding squared butt. A biconical perforation, 2 mm in diameter, is situated about 0.2 cm from the edge of the butt. Two series of shallow grooves, six on one edge and seven on the opposite edge, occur near the butt. They seem to have been worn rather than cut, but how they came about is unknown. There is a high degree of use polish overall.

Provenience:
   Site 264, Basket Maker III - Pueblo I

Punches

Thirty finished, complete artifacts fashioned from long bones of mammals are characterized by a short, tapering, symmetrical or asymmetrical, broad or sturdy point, with round or blunted tip ground and smoothed at the distal end, and a ground and smoothed butt at the other end (fig. 13h and i). Called "punches," they are listed by species and elements on the opposite page.

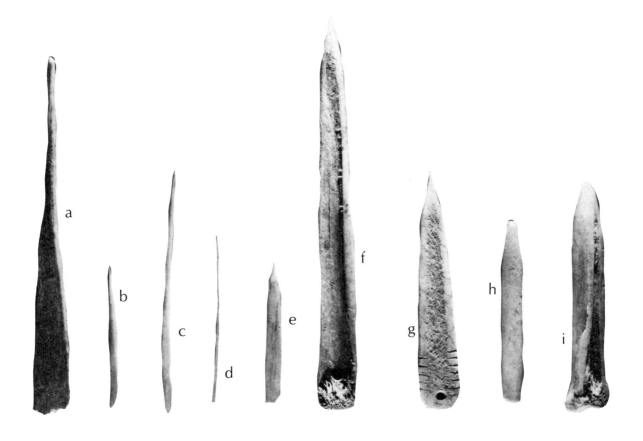

Figure 13. Bone awl spatulas, a-e; bodkins, f and g; and punches, h and i. Length of f is 14.9 cm.

Figure	Species	Element	Count
	Odocoileus hemionus, mule deer	metatarsal, proximal end	2
	Artiodactyl	tibia	1
		metatarsal	1
13i		metapodial	6
13h	Unidentifiable		20
		Total	30

Measurements: The 30 specimens range in overall length from 5 to 13.6 cm. The tips of at least 11 specimens show a high degree of use or wear polish. This suggests that these tools, if indeed they were "punches," were used on no tougher materials than wood or other bones.

Provenience:

Pink Arrow, Pueblo III - IV	3
Awatovi, Pueblo III - V	27
Total	30

Needles

The largest class of bone tools in the present collection, barring awls, is needles, of which 19 are complete (except for the tip in four cases) and 19 are fragments of various kinds. Made from long bone splinters of unidentifiable mammals, these superbly crafted tools — and also the pins described below — are beyond question among the most exquisite *functional* objects ever recovered from the earth. Six groups of needles are recognized for descriptive purposes.

GROUP A

Needles with eye and notch. Thirteen specimens are complete except, in three cases, for the tip. The ten fully intact specimens range in length from 4.5 to 14.1 cm. Shaft widths of the 13 needles vary from 0.3 to 0.6 cm, and thicknesses from 0.2 to 0.35 cm. The eye of the needles of this group is a round to oval perforation drilled in a straight or conical manner; it measures 1 to 5 mm in maximum diameter and is situated in the proximal end or butt of the needle at a distance ranging between 0.35 and 1.6 cm from the inner angle of the V-shaped notch in the very end of the needle. The V-notch varies from 1 to 5 mm in width and depth, respectively (fig. 14a). In ten of the specimens of Group A — none of which is illustrated — a minuscule groove connects the eye and the inner angle of the V-notch on both faces of the needle except in one instance. The significance of these narrow, shallow grooves is not known.

GROUP B

Needles with notch but no eye. Six specimens are complete except, in one case, for the tip. The five fully intact specimens range in length from 7.6 to 11.2 cm. Shaft widths of the six needles range from 0.3 to 0.6 cm, and thicknesses from 0.2 to 0.5 cm. The V-notch in the needles of this group varies from 1 to 2 mm in width and from 1 to 4 mm in depth (fig. 14b). A narrow, shallow groove, 0.8 cm long, similar to the grooves found in needles of Group A, occurs in one face of one needle of Group B.

GROUP C

Needle with eye but no notch. Both the proximal end, or butt, and the tapering pointed end of the single needle set off as "Group C" are missing, so that the overall length of this specimen is more than 6.7 cm. The shaft is 0.4 cm wide and 0.2 cm thick. The eye is a biconically drilled, round perforation, 1 mm in diameter, situated 0.9 cm from the stub of the broken proximal end.

GROUP D

Needles broken through the eye. The 11 specimens in this group have been broken, supposedly in the course of hard use, transversely through the eye of the needle in each instance. The round eye was drilled in either a straight or conical manner in the center of each face of the shaft and varies from 1 to 3 mm in diameter. Shaft widths range from 0.3 to 0.5 cm and thicknesses from 0.2 to 0.35 cm. Shallow, narrow grooves were noted in ten of the 13 needles of Group A; they ran between the V-notch in the butt and the eye. Similar grooves are present in seven of the 11 needles of Group D — on both faces in five cases and in one face in only two instances. But in these needles, the grooves run from the eye toward the point for distances varying from 0.2 to 1.4 cm. The origin of these grooves also eludes comprehension.

GROUP E

Distal fragments of needles. There are six specimens. The tapering points, with shaft widths ranging from 0.3 to 0.4 cm and thicknesses from 0.2 to 0.3 cm, have sharp tips in three cases, flaked back tips in two cases, and a blunted tip in one instance. Three specimens show a high degree of use polish at the tip.

GROUP F

Medial fragment of a needle. The single needle placed in this group lacks both proximal and distal ends. The shaft

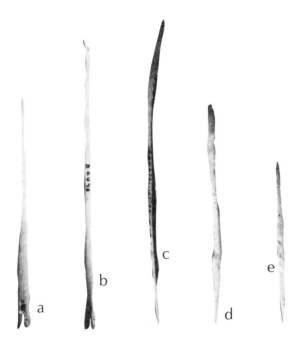

Figure 14. Bone needles, a and b; pins, c-e; and spatulas, f-i. Length of f is 12.6 cm.

measures slightly more than 0.4 cm in diameter and shows a high degree of use polish.

Provenience for Needle class:

Awatovi, Pueblo III	2
Awatovi, Pueblo IV	11
Awatovi, Pueblo V	24
Unassigned	1
Total	38

Pins

Nine exceptionally delicate pointed objects, made from splinters of bone of unidentifiable mammals or birds and finely ground and smoothed, are designated as "pins." Eight of them are single pointed (fig. 14c and d). The pointed end of one of the eight has been broken off. The other seven intact specimens range in length from 7.4 to 11.8 cm. The shafts of the eight pins vary in width from 0.3 to 0.65 cm and in thickness from 0.2 to 0.35 cm. In three cases, the tip shows a high degree of use polish.

One pin is bipointed (fig. 14e). It measures 5.8 by 0.3 by 0.2 cm and is flat oval in cross section. One end has a short tapering point, 1.3 cm in length, with a slightly blunted tip; the other end has a long tapering point, 2.6 cm in length, with a slightly rounded tip.

Provenience:

Awatovi, Pueblo III	4
Awatovi, Pueblo IV	1
Awatovi, Pueblo V	4
Total	9

Spatulas

Fourteen relatively long and slender tools in the collection having a bifacially beveled, sharp, even, single-end blade or similar double-end blades, evidently used for precise cutting purposes, are designated "spatulas," a term commonly applied in the literature to such artifacts.

Of the spatulas with single-end blade, six are complete and six have the proximal end or butt broken off. Two of the complete specimens were made from the radius of a large artiodactyl (fig. 14f) and the tibia of *Lepus californicus*, black-tailed jackrabbit (fig. 14g), but the other four complete spatulas (fig. 14h and i) and the six fragmentary single-end blade spatulas were made from bone splinters of unidentifiable mammals. The six complete specimens range in length from 8.3 to 17 cm. The width of the 12 spatulas varies from 0.75 to 4.3 cm, and the thickness from 0.2 to 1.5 cm. Blade widths range from 0.75 to 4.2 cm. The edge of the blade is sharp in three cases, blunted or dulled in nine cases. Four spatulas show a high degree of wear polish overall.

The other two spatulas have double-end blades. One of them, measuring 9.5 by 1.1 by 0.3 cm, has a blade with a convex edge, dulled by use, at one end, and a blade with an oblique edge, nicked and dulled by use, at the opposite end. The other specimen, 12.1 by 1.45 by 0.2 cm has a blade with an oblique convex edge, dulled by use, at one end, and a blade with a slightly concave edge, blunted by use, at the other end.

Provenience:

Awatovi, Pueblo III	2
Awatovi, Pueblo IV	5
Awatovi, Pueblo V	7
Total	14

End Scrapers

Twenty-five complete and eight fragmentary tools in the collection fashioned from various elements of identifiable mammals and unidentifiable mammals or birds are designated "end scrapers." They are thought to have been employed mainly to remove flesh from hides, particularly deer hides, and are often called "fleshers."

In the single example of an end scraper made from the tibia of *Odocoileus hemionus,* mule deer, the distal joint is unmodified and the whole shaft has been pared and ground to a convex edge, about 2.2 cm wide, which is nicked by use. The overall length of the tool is 22 cm (fig. 15a).

In the one complete specimen of an end scraper made from the (left) humerus of a mule deer or possibly bighorn sheep, the distal joint is somewhat worn, broken, or rotted off, and the whole shaft has been cut transversely on the ventral face to produce a broad, square blade, 3.4 cm wide, with rounded corners and a unifacially beveled edge slightly dulled by wear. The overall length of this scraper is 13.5 cm (fig. 15b). Another end scraper, 7.5 cm in length, with a broad, convex, unifacially beveled edge slightly more than 3.3 cm in width (fig. 15c), appears to be the blade fragment of a humerus scraper similar to the one just described above.

There are three complete and five fragmentary whole long bone end scrapers. Two of the complete specimens have been identified as a radius of *Lepus californicus,* black-tailed jackrabbit, and a femur of *Canis,* sp. The third complete specimen and the five distal end fragments were not identifiable. The three complete specimens range in overall length from 7.8 to 10 cm. The eight whole bone end scrapers may be grouped according to the characteristics of their working edges, as follows:

Unifacially beveled convex edge: two specimens; 0.6 and 1.2 cm wide
Unifacially beveled concave edge: one specimen; 2.4 cm wide
Unifacially beveled straight edge; five specimens; 0.4 to 4.2 cm wide.

There are eight complete and one fragmentary rib end scrapers. All are made from the midsections of ribs. One of the complete specimens is from the rib of a large artiodactyl (fig. 15d). The complete rib end scrapers range in overall length from 4.6 to 18.8 cm. The nine specimens vary in width from 1.2 to 4.2 cm, and in thickness from 0.4 to 0.65 cm. It was observed that the working end of each rib end scraper had been worn rather smooth, supposedly by use.

Finally, there are 13 end scrapers developed on a variety of bone splinters — nine splinters of long bones of mammals, only two of which have been identified as a metatarsal of *Odocoileus hemionus,* mule deer, and a metapodial of artiodactyl; two splinters of scapulae, one of which has been identified as *Ovis aries,* domestic sheep; the splinter of a nasal bone of *Ovis;* and the splinter of an innominate of a small mammal or bird. These end scrapers range in overall length from 4.6 to 11.4 cm, and they vary greatly in shape as well as size. Many of them show considerable wear on one or more sides in addition to smoothing on the working end.

Provenience:

Site 111, early Pueblo II	1
Awatovi, Pueblo III	13
Awatovi, Pueblo IV	6
Awatovi, Pueblo V	13
Total	33

Miscellaneous Utility

There are twenty complete or virtually complete and three fragmentary artifacts in the collection that seem to have served, or at least to have been designed to serve, functional purposes and yet do not fit into any of the classes of tools described above. They are classified here as "miscellaneous utility."

SERRATED TOOLS

The concave edge of the midsection of a left (?) rib of *Equus* cf. *caballus,* probably mule, measuring 20.9 by 3.1 by 1 cm, bears irregular notches, 1 to 1.5 mm deep, which have been worn smooth with use (fig. 16a). This implement *may* have been a sword used to beat down wefts in small looms.

A fragmentary object made from a long bone splinter of an unidentifiable mammal, rough at one end and broken at the other, measuring 5.9 by 1.3 by 0.6 cm, has four V-shaped notches on one side and five on the other, 0.5 to 2 mm deep, with rounded edges (fig. 16b). The worn and broken condition of the specimen suggests that it was once part of a larger tool.

A small intact tool of trapezoidal shape, made from bone of an unidentifiable mammal, measures 1.6 cm

Figure 15. Bone end scrapers. Length of a is 22 cm.

across the upper edge, 3.3 cm across the lower edge, 2.5 cm between these edges, and 0.3 cm thick. It has seven V-notches in the center of the lower edge, 1 mm deep (fig. 16c). This tidy instrument may have been used in the decorative arts.

A tough and durable drill or reamer can be identified — at least in my view — in the canine tooth of *Canis* sp., which has three shallow, parallel grooves in the enamel just above the ground tip and two deeper grooves on the opposite side of the tooth (fig. 16f).

GOUGES (?)

Ten complete tools were possible gouges. They were made from several elements of different mammalian species. This can be indicated most economically in tabular form below:

The illustrated specimen (fig. 16d) measures 10.7 by 1.4 by 0.7 cm. It has been finished overall by grinding and smoothing. One end (top) is cut transversely, the opposite end is beveled unifacially on the convex face (the face

Figure	Species	Element	Count
16d	*Canis* cf. *latrans,* coyote	radius	1
	Antilocapra americana, pronghorn	radius-ulna, distal end	1
	Odocoileus hemionus, mule deer	ulna, proximal end	1
	Ovis aries, domestic sheep/goat	radius, distal	1
		tibia, distal	1
	Ovis (?)	ulna, proximal	1
	Equus caballus, horse	splint bone	1
	Artiodactyl	humerus, distal	1
		radius	1
		tibia	1
		Total	10

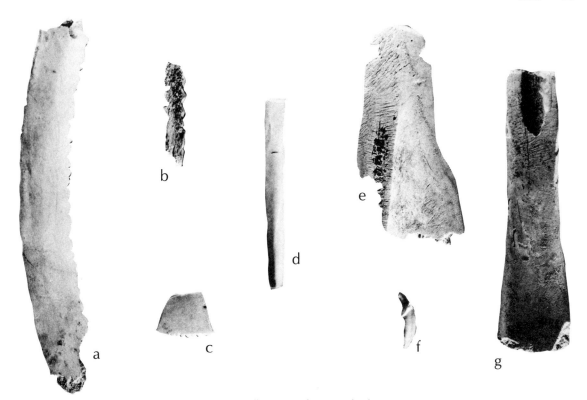

Figure 16. Bone miscellaneous utility. Length of a is 20.9 cm.

shown in the illustration). The other nine specimens range in length from 6.9 to 16.3 cm. Each of them has a blunted or scraperlike working end.

HOE-BLADE (?)

A fragment of a possible hoe-blade is made from the scapula of a large mammal, comparable to bison. The fragment has a carved semicircular knob with notches on each side measuring 1 cm wide by 0.5 cm deep and 1.3 cm wide by 0.3 cm deep, respectively (fig. 16e). This knob may have been provided for attaching the hoe-blade to a wooden handle at right angles.

CHISELS (?)

A complete artifact, measuring 15.4 by 4.1 by 3 cm, is made from the midsection of a radius of a large mammal, comparable to bison. It is cut transversely and ground at the narrower end or butt and is nicked and chipped at the wider end, as if from use as a chisel (fig. 16g). Two complete, slightly smaller artifacts, 11.8 and 11.4 cm in length, not identified as to species but similar in appearance to the illustrated specimen, may be considered to be chisels also.

HANDLES (?)

One complete artifact, made from the distal end of a tibia of artiodactyl, measures 8 by 2.7 by 2.1 cm. The distal end and the shaft are ground on the edges. The other artifact, made from the midsection of a rib of artiodactyl, measures 6.15 by 2.65 by 1 cm. One end is nicely ground. At a distance of 0.4 cm in from this end runs a lengthwise groove, 2 mm wide and 13 mm deep. Both artifacts are provisionally regarded as handles.

Lastly, the artifacts described below resist even such tentative pigeonholing as I have suggested for those described previously in this section.

1. Middle portion of a rib of artiodactyl, 23.2 by 3.9 by 1.6 cm, roughly rounded at the wider end, with a recess, 0.6 cm deep, gouged out and ground at the narrower end.

2. Splinter of a metapodial of artiodactyl, 14.3 by 1.5 by 0.8 cm. Ground articular end has V-notch in center, 6 mm wide and 5 mm deep, which is not clearly intentional.

3. Long bone splinter fragment of unidentifiable mammal, ground on one convex end, and completely covered with pink pigment.

Provenience for Miscellaneous Utility class:

Awatovi, Pueblo III	5
Awatovi, Pueblo IV	5
Awatovi, Pueblo V	12
Unassigned	1
Total	23

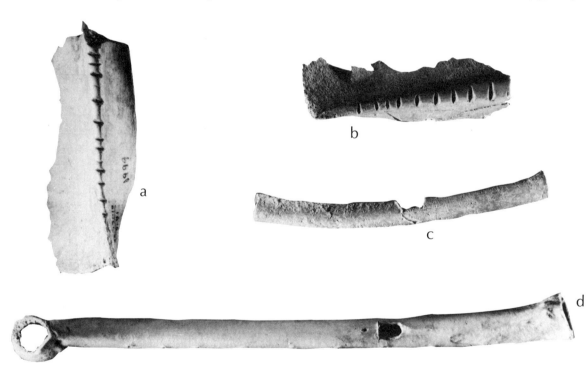

Figure 17. Bone sounding-rasps, a and b; and whistles, c and d. Length of d is 19.5 cm.

MUSICAL INSTRUMENTS

Sounding-Rasps

Seventeen portions of scapulae bearing V-notches are recognizable as sounding-rasps, which have been used by Puebloan peoples for centuries as simple percussive instruments in ceremonial rituals. All but four of them have been identified below.

One of the two illustrated specimens (fig. 17a), measuring 8.6 by 3.3 by 1.5 cm, has 12 short, shallow V-notches cut irregularly in the dorsal (?) border. They have been so well worn by use that they now produce only a fair degree of sound. In the other illustrated example (fig. 17b), one end has seemingly been cut, whereas the opposite end and lower body have been roughly broken. Measuring 7.4 cm in length and 2.2 cm in width, this specimen has a series of nine deep V-notches in the ventral edge of the upper border. The volume of sound was good.

The other 15 sounding-rasps range in length from 3.6 to 15.6 cm and in width from 1 to 6.9 cm. I tested the 17 sounding-rasps for sound (or noise) capacity and rated them: uncertain or poor, 3; fair, 4; and good, 10.

Provenience:

Awatovi, Pueblo III	3
Awatovi, Pueblo IV	6
Awatovi, Pueblo V	8
Total	17

Figure	Species	Element	Count
17a	*Antilocapra americana,* pronghorn	scapula, side?	1
		scapula, right	1
		scapula, left	2
	Odocoileus hemionus, mule deer	scapula, right	2
	Artiodactyl	scapula, right	2
17b		scapula, left	1
		scapula, side?	4
		Total	13

Whistles

Of four artifacts in the collection characterized by a hollow shaft and an opening in the shaft, two are pretty certainly whistles and two may or may not be whistles. One of the definite whistles is made from the middle section of a radius of *Aquila chrysaëtos,* golden eagle (fig. 17c). The ends were cut off squarely and ground, but the sides of the bone are unmodified. An oblong opening, 0.85 cm long and 0.4 cm wide, was cut into one side at a distance of 5.4 cm from one end and 4.8 cm from the other. It was found that this small whistle sounded a strong high note.

The other unmistakable whistle is made from an ulna of *Aquila chrysaëtos,* golden eagle (fig. 17d). One end was cut at right angles and ground, and the other end was cut obliquely and ground, but the sides are unmodified. A subrectangular opening, 0.9 cm long and 0.45 cm wide, was cut into one side at a distance of 6.1 cm from the obliquely cut end. Experimentally, it was found that this whistle sounded a strong medium-high note.

One of the provisional whistles, made from a bird (?) bone, with cut and ground ends, has an irregular opening, 0.9 cm long and 0.3 cm wide, cut into one side at a distance of 4.1 cm from one end and 5.2 cm from the other. When sounded, this specimen produced a high note of only fair quality.

The other uncertain whistle, made of the long bone of mammal or bird, has irregularly cut and ground ends and an oval opening in a flat side, from 0.25 to 0.5 cm in diameter. When sounded, this specimen produced such meager sound that perhaps it should be classed as a tubular bead rather than a musical instrument.

Provenience:

Awatovi, Pueblo III	3
Awatovi, Pueblo V	1
Total	4

ORNAMENTS

Tubular Beads — Individual

Two hundred and four individual tubular bone beads in the collection were made of mammal or bird bone. None of the 85 bird bone beads were identifiable as to species and only 13 of the 119 mammal bone beads (fig. 18a-h) were identifiable, as follows:

Species	Element	Count
Lynx rufus, bobcat	humerus	1
	radius	1
	femur	2
Canis cf. latrans, coyote	humerus	1
	femur	1
	tibia	2
Canis, sp. dog or coyote	femur	2
	tibia	2
Artiodactyl	tibia	1
	Total	13

Figure 18. Bone tubular beads, a-h; pendants or beads, i-o; and gaming pieces or dice, p and q. Length of a is 8.8 cm.

The tubular beads are cylindrical in shape and range in length from 0.9 to 13 cm, and in diameter from 0.45 to 2.4 cm. The ends are cut squarely, or beveled at one or both ends, and ground. In almost all cases, the surfaces of the beads are unmodified but occasionally they show slight wear polish.

Exceptions to the monotonous uniformity of the tubular beads exhibited by the examples illustrated in figure 18a and e-g, are four beads with a circular perforation in the middle of the bead (fig. 18b; this has a perforation in opposite faces of the bead, unlike the other three); a bead with notches at each end (fig. 18c); a slightly tapering cylindrical bead with an overall, shallowly carved herringbone motif (fig. 18d); three beads with an encircling incised line (fig. 18h); a bead with a pair of finely incised lines at each end, and a bead with incised Vs and a deeply incised line at each end.

Provenience:

Awatovi, Pueblo III	55
Awatovi, Pueblo IV	45
Awatovi, Pueblo V	82
Kawaika-a, Pueblo III - IV	2
Pink Arrow, Pueblo III - IV	10
Unassigned	9
Not known	1
Total	204

Tubular and Flat Rectangular Beads — in Eight Clusters

Two hundred and eighty-two tubular beads and five flat rectangular beads were found in eight clusters of different provenience at Awatovi. They are best described, it seems to me, cluster by cluster:

1. Twenty-four short bird bone tubular beads, 2.6 to 3.95 cm in length and 0.4 to 0.6 cm in diameter, with the ends cut transversely or obliquely, the surfaces slightly smoothed or ground; apparently representing all or part of a necklace or bracelet.

2. Five short mammal bone tubular beads, 1.4 to 1.6 cm in length and 1.2 to 1.35 cm in diameter, with the ends irregular and unground or ground down, the surfaces unmodified; and one short bird bone tubular bead, 1.8 cm long and 1.2 cm in diameter, with the ends irregularly cut and ground, the surface unmodified. This cluster was found with a burial (no. 42).

3. One bird bone (?) tubular bead and two mammal bone (?) tubular beads, all fragmentary, with unmodified surfaces.

4. Twenty-six short mammal bone (?) tubular beads, ranging from 0.8 cm in length and 0.5 cm in diameter to 1.4 cm in length to 0.6 cm in diameter, with the ends cut transversely and ground and the surfaces unmodified; and 11 short bird bone (?) tubular beads, ranging from 0.9 cm in length and 0.4 cm in diameter to 1.3 cm in length and 0.6 cm in diameter, with the ends cut transversely and ground and the surfaces unmodified.

5. Five short mammal bone (?) tubular beads, heavily burned, mostly calcined, (two of which are strung with burned cordage), ranging from 2 cm in length and 1.7 cm in diameter to 3 cm in length and 1.3 cm in diameter, with the ends cut transversely or beveled; and five short bird bone (?) tubular beads, also heavily burned, mostly calcined, ranging from 1.3 cm in length and 1.2 cm in diameter to 3 cm in length and 1.8 cm in diameter, with the ends cut transversely and ground (?). This cluster was found with a burial (no. 57).

6. Nine short tubular beads of mammal or bird leg bone, ranging from 1.9 cm in length and 1 cm in diameter to 2.6 cm in length and 1.2 cm in diameter. The ends are cut transversely or beveled and ground down and the surfaces are unmodified.

7. Nine long tubular beads of bird bone, ranging from 8.1 cm in length and 0.8 cm in diameter to 9.6 cm in length and 0.9 cm in diameter. The ends are cut transversely or irregularly and ground, and the surfaces are slightly polished by wear.

8. This cluster of 189 specimens consists of:

a. 130 small tubular beads of mammal (?) long bones, ranging from 0.8 cm in length and 0.4 cm in diameter to 1.4 cm in length and 0.7 cm in diameter, with transversely cut and ground or unground ends and unmodified surfaces;

b. 43 small tubular beads of bird (?) long bones, ranging from 0.8 cm in length and 0.4 cm in diameter to 1.6 cm in length and 0.7 cm in diameter, with transversely cut and ground ends and unmodified surfaces;

c. 11 short tubular beads of mammal or bird long bones, ranging from 0.7 cm in length and 0.4 cm in diameter to 1.1 cm in length and 0.55 cm in diameter. The ends are cut transversely and ground and the surfaces are unmodified;

d. 5 flat rectangular beads made from mammal (?) rib bones or flattish long bones, with the ends cut transversely and ground. Each bead has a circular or oval perforation, 3 to 4 mm in maximum diameter, in the convex face only.

The last and largest cluster was found on the wrist of a burial (no. 15).

Provenience:

Awatovi, Pueblo III	1
Awatovi, Pueblo IV	1
Awatovi, Pueblo V	6
Total	8

Pendants or Beads — Individual

There are 28 individual pendants or beads in the collection. Eight of these are rectangular, longitudinally split sections of unidentifiable mammal bones. The example illustrated (fig. 18i) measures 4.5 by 1.1 by 0.55 cm. The ends were cut transversely and ground. The pendant is highly polished and has two conical perforations, one near each end, 3.5 and 4 mm in diameter. The other seven specimens of this group range in length from 1.5 to 4.4 cm, in width from 1 to 2.2 cm, and in thickness from 0.1 to 0.3 cm. The pattern of conical or, more often, biconical perforations varies from one and two at each end, through two incomplete ones at one end, to three at one end and none at the opposite end, with diameters ranging from 2 to 3.5 mm.

Eleven pendants or beads are rectangular, long bone splinters of unidentifiable mammals. They range in length from 2.1 to 4.4 cm, in width from 1 to 3.5 cm, and in thickness from 0.1 to 0.3 cm. The ends are generally cut transversely and ground, and the surfaces are either unmodified or slightly smoothed. One pendant (fig. 18j) has a pair of biconical perforations, 2.5 and 3 mm in diameter near one end, and two lightly incised oblique lines with a shallow circular dot, 1.5 mm in diameter in the middle, just below the center of the piece. Three other specimens have a pair of biconical perforations, 2 to 3 mm in diameter, at one end, like the illustrated example, and two of these have in addition incised lines at the same end as the perforations and one has a pair of oblique incised lines near the middle of the piece. Two specimens have two pairs of biconical perforations, 2 mm in diameter, at each end (fig. 18k and m) and two have a tiny notch in the middle of each end (fig. 18l). A single pendant (fig. 18n) has three shallow vertical incised lines and a deep horizontal incised line at each end, and one pendant has an almond-shaped perforation, 2 mm by 4 mm, near one edge.

Four pendants or beads — three complete and one fragment — are made from parts of crania of unidentifiable mammals or birds. A complete oval specimen, with cut and ground edges and unmodified surfaces, measures 4.1 by 3.6 by 0.2 cm. It has a round, biconical perforation, 2 mm in diameter, situated 0.5 cm in from one edge. Two complete subcircular pendants, with cut and ground edges, measure 2.6 by 2.4 by 0.3 cm and 3 by 3.3 by 0.2 cm, respectively. The former has a round, biconical perforation, 2 to 3 mm in diameter, 0.4 cm in from the edges; the latter has twin perforations, 2.5 mm in diameter, 0.4 and 0.5 cm in from one edge (fig. 18o). The edge fragment has a subcircular, biconical perforation, 2 mm in diameter, 0.6 cm in from one edge.

The vertebra of an artiodactyl, with ground edges and unmodified surfaces, has an oval, biconical perforation, 3 mm in diameter, situated 0.65 cm in from one end.

Part of the cranium of a turtle, discoidal in shape, has apparently been prepared for use as a pendant or bead by grinding and polishing of the edges and the convex surface.

Finally, there are three canine teeth of *Cervus canadensis*, wapiti, each of which having a round, biconically drilled perforation, 3 to 4 mm in diameter, in two cases, or 4 to 5 mm, in one case, situated near the root of the tooth.

Provenience:

Awatovi, Pueblo III	5
Awatovi, Pueblo IV	6
Awatovi, Pueblo V	16
Kawaika-a, Pueblo III - IV	1
Total	28

Pendants or Beads — In One Cluster

The collection includes one cluster of seven end fragments of rectangular pendants or beads made from rib sections (?) of unidentifiable mammals. Measuring 1 to 1.2 cm in width and 0.15 to 0.2 cm in thickness, each specimen has a pair of round biconically drilled perforations, 1 mm in diameter, near the extant end, and five of the seven pendants have a row of tiny incisions at this end also, on the convex face only. This cluster was found with a burial (no. 92).

Provenience: Awatovi, Pueblo V

OTHER ARTIFACTS

Gaming Pieces or Dice

Twenty artifacts in the collection do not seem to match up with any of the classes of material described previously in this paper. Most of the specimens, 14 in number, resemble the one illustrated in figure 18p: made of long bone splinters of unidentifiable mammals, they are subrectangular in shape, that is to say, the ends and sides may vary from straight to convex to tapering, and combinations thereof. Ends, sides, and one or both surfaces are ground and sometimes polished, and the surfaces are invariably plain. These specimens range in length from 1.5 to 5.4 cm, in width from 0.8 to 1.8 cm, and in thickness from 0.15 to 0.4 cm.

An elongated oval specimen, measuring 7.2 by 1.3 by 0.4 cm, was made from a section of longitudinally split rib of unidentifiable mammal. The convex ends and sides were ground and polished, and the convex face shows wear polish, but cancellous tissue is evident on the inner, concave face. The outer face is plain.

A subtriangular specimen, made from a long bone splinter of unidentifiable mammal, measures 4.5 by 1.6 by 0.4 cm. The ends, sides, and faces are ground and polished. Again the outer face is plain.

One subrectangular specimen is made from a long bone splinter of unidentifiable bird. The piece measures 2.3 by 0.9 by 0.35 cm; the ends, sides, and faces are ground and smoothed. The surfaces are plain.

One subrectangular specimen, made of a long bone splinter of unidentifiable mammal or bird, measures 2.2 by 1.2 by 0.25 cm. The straight ends and sides and the convex faces are ground and polished. Once again the surfaces are plain.

An oval specimen with flat faces, nicely ground and polished, measures 2.8 by 1.2 by 0.2 cm (fig. 18q). One face bears many crisscross incisions awash with red pigment (?).

Finally, a hemispherical object of tooth enamel (?), 1 cm in diameter, with ground and polished edges, has an incised cross and a faint depression, 1.5 mm in diameter, at the crossover, in the flat face.

If most of the little pieces described had not been *plain* but had borne marks, however cryptic, like the two just mentioned, I would feel no hesitation in proposing that these artifacts were gaming pieces or dice. Still, after considerable thought, I have no better suggestion to offer.

Provenience:

Site 264, Basket Maker III - Pueblo I	1
Site 4A, Basket Maker III - Pueblo III	1
Awatovi, Pueblo III	3
Awatovi, Pueblo IV	2
Awatovi, Pueblo V	8
Pink Arrow, Pueblo III - IV	2
Kawaika-a, Pueblo III - IV	3
Total	20

Stock

Seventy items in the collection are artifacts in the broad sense of being pieces altered by the hand of man. They may be dubbed bone "stock." They are of interest for two reasons: (a) they enlarge the faunal inventory of the sites of the Jeddito District since a high proportion of them are the identifiable articular ends of bones from which unidentifiable shaft sections had been cut off; and (b) they show evidences of technics employed in cutting shaft sections from long bones for use as tubular beads and other artifacts.

Nineteen specimens of mammal bone and one of bird bone were not identifiable as to species. The rest were identified as follows:

Figure	Species	Element	Count
MAMMALS			
19a	Canis, sp. dog or coyote	right humerus, proximal end	1
		left humerus, proximal	1
		right humerus, distal end	3
		left humerus, distal	3
		right femur, distal	1
		left femur, proximal	2
		femur, distal	1
	Canis cf. latrans, coyote	radius, proximal	1
		right femur, proximal	2
		tibia, proximal	1
		tibia, distal	1
	Canis cf. familiaris, domestic dog	right humerus, distal	1
		right tibia, proximal	1
		metapodial	1
	Lynx rufus, bobcat	right femur, distal	1
		tibia	1
	Lepus californicus, black-tailed jackrabbit	radius	1
19b		left femur, proximal	1
	Odocoileus hemionus, mule deer	metatarsal	1
	Antilocapra americana, pronghorn	radius-ulna, distal	1
		femur, proximal	1
		tibia, distal	2
		metacarpal	2
		metatarsal, distal	3
	Ovis canadensis, bighorn sheep	radius, proximal	1
	Artiodactyl	rib	4
		radius	1
		femur, proximal	1

BIRDS

19c	*Aquila chrysaëtos*, golden eagle	right coracoid, proximal	1
		left humerus, distal	1
		left ulna, proximal	1
		left femur, distal	1
		left tibiotarsus, proximal	1
19d	*Grus canadensis*, sandhill crane	right tarsometatarsus, distal	1
		right tibiotarsus	1
19e		left ulna, distal	1
19f	*Pelecanus erythrorhynchos*, white pelican	left humerus, proximal	1
		Total	50

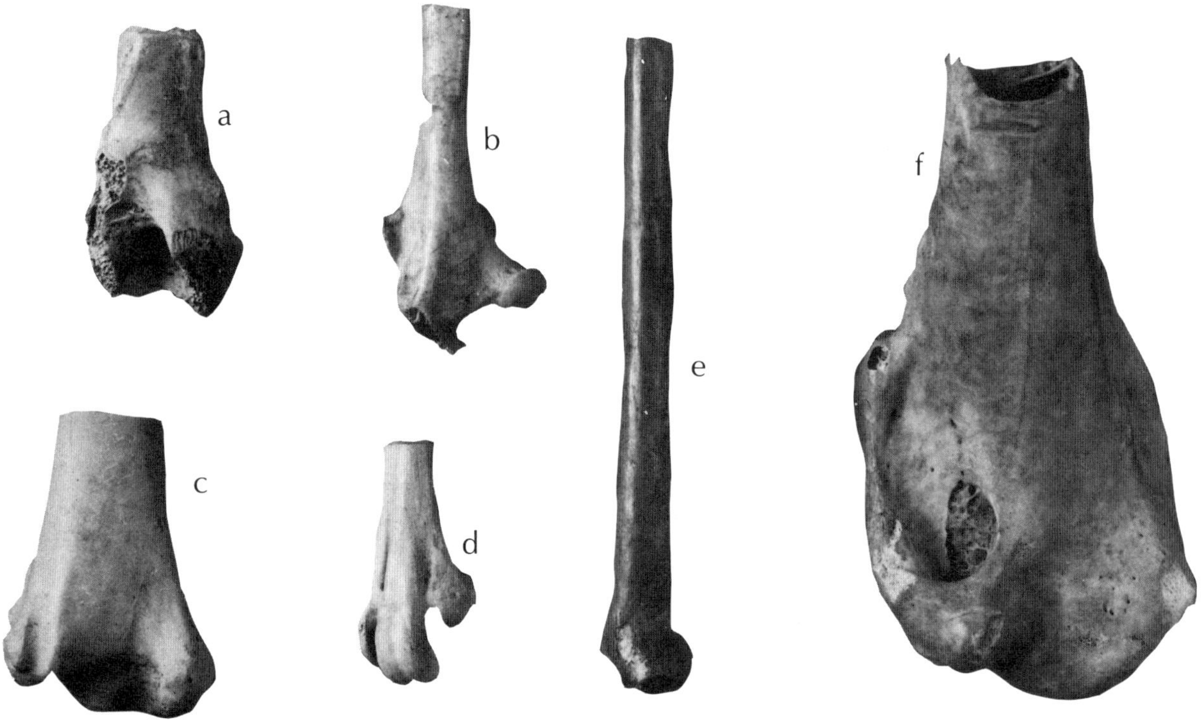

Figure 19. Bone stock from which tubular beads or other artifacts may have been derived. Length of f is 10.2 cm.

The technics employed in cutting shaft sections from long bones transversely were (1) sawing and breaking, as shown by specimens in figure 19a-d and f and (2) whittling and breaking, as shown by the specimen in figure 19b. The sawing of a given piece appears to have been accomplished by applying a small, fine-grained sandstone saw to the bone at several places around its circumference. The characteristic "bevel" edge adjacent to the "ragged" broken edge of the bone is one-half of the V-groove produced by the sandstone saw. The whittling of a given piece seems to have been done by a flaked stone knife or scraper.

Longitudinal cutting of shaft sections involved the same technics as transverse cutting.

Provenience:

Site 103, Pueblo II	1
Awatovi, Pueblo III	31
Awatovi, Pueblo IV	12
Awatovi, Pueblo V	22
Pink Arrow, Pueblo III - IV	2
Unassigned	1
Not known	1
Total	70

Artifacts of Antler

Antler used by the people of Awatovi and their neighbors for artifacts was the by-product of hunting and was rather easily turned into flakers of flint tools and other very useful implements. Its single drawback from the prehistorian's point-of-view — as inferred from the small proportion of antler artifacts compared to those of bone in the present assemblage — is its apparent tendency to disintegrate and disappear in open, desiccated sites such as Awatovi.

For convenience, the antler artifacts from the Jeddito District have been grouped as follows:

Classification and Tabulation

Awls	5
Flakers	53
Wedges	11
Handles	16
Miscellaneous Artifacts	18
Total	103

Awls

There are five antler awls in the collection — two complete, one distal fragment, and two proximal or butt fragments.

One of the complete awls is 9.9 cm in overall length and has a long tapering point about 5.2 cm in length with a rounded tip and five shallow incisions on one face just above the tip. The other intact awl measures 6.5 cm in overall length and has a short point, 1.8 cm in length, with a sharp tip.

The distal fragment has a short point, 1.1 cm in length, with the tip flaked back and blunted. One butt fragment is rounded by grinding, the other is asymmetrically rounded at the end and is ground and smoothed on the sides.

Provenience:

Awatovi, Pueblo III	3
Awatovi, Pueblo IV	1
Awatovi, Pueblo V	1
Total	5

Flakers

By all odds, the most numerous antler implements in the collection are flakers, or modified deer tines supposedly used mainly in the pressure flaking of flint stone tools. Forty-four flakers are complete and nine are fragmentary.

Two of the intact flakers have both ends tapered to blunt points. One of these (fig. 20g) is 15.6 cm in length and 1.1 cm in diameter, and the blunt points are about 0.8 cm long. The other bipointed flaker measures 13.3 by 1 by 0.35 cm. Both flakers are extensively ground and, being very nearly straight, are greatly modified tines.

Forty-two complete flakers have one point each, which is usually blunted. They range in length from 3.2 to 11.9 cm. Sixteen are four-sided (fig. 20h) and range in width from 0.9 to 2.8 cm, and in thickness from 0.7 to 1.9 cm. The rest, 26 in number, are tapered cylindrically (fig. 20i) and range in maximum diameter from 0.6 to 2.5 cm. The natural smoothness and contours of the tines were retained, and only their very tips show signs of chipping and blunting from use. The single exception to this is the series of short incisions found along one edge of the flaker illustrated in figure 20h; the significance of these markings is not known.

Of the nine fragmentary flakers, one has a broken tip, two have broken bases, one is broken at both ends, and five are split longitudinally.

Provenience:

Awatovi, Pueblo III	21
Awatovi, Pueblo IV	4
Awatovi, Pueblo V	27
Unassigned	1
Total	53

Wedges

Two intact artifacts and nine very fragile ones having one end or one short side unifacially or bifacially beveled to a rounded or blunted edge may have served, or may have been designed to serve, as wedges. One of the intact

Figure 20. Antler artifacts: iron awl handle, a; pipe, b; tubular bead, c; wedge, d; knife handles, e,f, and k; flakers, g-i; and drift, j. Length of g is 15.6 cm.

specimens, apparently made from a bez antler (fig. 20d) is 8.4 cm in length. One end has a unifacially beveled, rounded edge about 1.8 cm wide; the other end has been cut and irregularly nibbled off. The other specimens range in length from 5.3 to 18.3 cm, and their beveled edges range in width from 1.1 to 2.5 cm.

Provenience:

Awatovi, Pueblo III	3
Awatovi, Pueblo IV	3
Awatovi, Pueblo V	5
Total	11

Handles

Three kinds of handles made of antler are represented in the collection:

1. with hollowed out recess (fig. 20e): 9 specimens; overall length ranges from 4.3 to 14.4 cm, recess ranges from 1 to 5.2 cm in depth;

2. with slit in one end (fig. 20f): 2 specimens; one measures 9.7 cm in length and 2.1 cm in maximum diameter, and the slit is 0.3 cm wide; the other measures 5.2 by 2.2 by 1.6 cm, and the slit is 0.2 cm wide;

3. with perforation in one end (fig. 20k): 3 specimens; illustrated example has straight perforation, 0.3 cm in diameter, and slit at side for knife (?), 1.9 cm long and 0.3 cm wide; other two perforations are straight, 0.6 cm, and conical, 0.2 cm in diameter.

Two other antler handles are mere fragments.

Provenience:

Awatovi, Pueblo III	1
Awatovi, Pueblo V	13
Pink Arrow, Pueblo III - IV	2
Total	16

Miscellaneous Artifacts

The first item of the 18 odds and ends to be described in this final section is the nicely cut and smoothed, tapered antler handle of a small rusted iron or steel awl. The handle is 4.2 cm long and 1.5 cm in maximum diameter, and the awl extends 3 cm beyond the top of the handle (fig. 20a).

An antler pipe (fig. 20b), 4.4 cm in length and 2 cm in maximum diameter, shaped by cutting and grinding and slightly blackened by use, has been hollowed out to a depth of 2.5 cm. Another antler pipe is 7.2 cm long.

A very well finished tubular bead of antler, slightly tapered at each end, with a perforation reaching straight through it, measures 5.8 cm in length and 1.1 cm in maximum diameter (fig. 20c). A fragmentary tubular bead, the ends of which are missing, is 0.9 cm in diameter.

A section of antler beam, cut squarely at one end and rounded at the other, may nave been a smoother for use in ceramics and other arts (fig. 20j).

An elongated pendant or bead of antler, nicely finished, has a biconical perforation near one end, 2 mm in diameter.

Two antler tines, 3.4 and 3.8 cm in length, rounded at the narrower end, have been hollowed out for some unknown purpose.

There is a residuum of nine artifacts of antler that are so fragmentary that it is not possible to tell whether they were meant to be wedges, handles, or even something entirely different. They will have to be left in limbo.

Provenience:

Awatovi, Pueblo III	2
Awatovi, Pueblo IV	2
Awatovi, Pueblo V	14
Total	18

Discussion

Tabulations of the bone and antler artifacts from the Jeddito District show that the antler assemblage amounts to only a little over 6 percent of the bone items. This discrepancy may be ascribed not only to the fact that, as raw material, antler was far less abundant than bone, but also to the tendency for antler to disintegrate in dry places such as the open prehistoric village sites investigated by the Peabody Museum Awatovi Expedition in the Jeddito District.

Few antler artifacts compared to bone artifacts have also been reported from Aztec Ruin, New Mexico (Morris 1919, p. 43), the La Plata District in southwestern Colorado and northwestern New Mexico (Morris 1939, p. 123), Alkali Ridge, southeastern Utah (Brew 1946, pp. 244-245), Pueblo Bonito, New Mexico (Judd 1954), and Pueblo del Arroyo, New Mexico (Judd 1959). However, a relative abundance of antler artifacts in comparison to bone artifacts was reported from Pecos Pueblo in New Mexico by Kidder (1932) and from Hawikuh in New Mexico by Hodge (1920).

As far as the bone artifact assemblage from the Jeddito District is concerned, tools represent 61.5 percent, musical instruments 1 percent, ornaments 32 percent, and other artifacts 5.5 percent of the whole. The items in the antler artifact assemblage from the district were grouped into five classes, but categorization paralleling the bone artifact assemblage was not attempted because of the small counts and the fragmentary and uncertain identification of numerous specimens.

A comparison of the difference in the use of mammal and bird bone for awls in the large sample from Pecos Pueblo and the smaller one from the Jeddito District gives the following counts and percentages:

The predominance of mammal bone over bird bone for awls in each sample may reflect the greater availability of mammal bone relative to bird bone in these localities. Still there is the possibility that mammal bone was recognized as somewhat tougher and more durable than bird bone and was preferred for the varied and rugged tasks that awls were used for.

Several classes of bone artifacts, familiar in certain Great Plains contexts, were present in the Pecos Pueblo inventory but absent from that of the Jeddito District. These consist of objects of cancellous bone ("paint brushes"), perforated bone discs or spindle whorls, projectile points, and arrow-shaft "wrenches" (Kidder 1932, pp. 237-242, figs. 198-201). Whistles and sounding-rasps were shared traits, but the various flageolets found at Pecos (ibid., pp. 249-252, figs. 207-210) were not present at Awatovi and nearby sites. A class of bone artifacts found rather commonly in the Four Corners and upper San Juan regions but absent from both the Jeddito District and Pecos is made from the tibia of a small mammal — jackrabbit, cottontail, bobcat, or coyote. The articular surface of the proximal (upper) joint is planed off by grinding at right angles, the cancellous tissue is cored out, and a small perforation is drilled through one wall of the shaft near the distal joint. The only other modification may be some wear polish of the shaft. The purpose of these perforated tibias is not known for certain, but it is possible that, as tinklers or rattles, they were part of priests' costumes worn in ritual "dances" (Hayes and Lancaster 1975, p. 170).

Many of the functional bone tools in the assemblage from the Jeddito District were superbly finished — notably the needles, pins, and spatulas — but, strangely, only one such

Bone Awls

			Count		Percentage
Pecos Pueblo	Mammal bone		2,226		89.8
(Kidder 1932)	Bird bone		253		10.2
		Total	2,479	Total	100.0
Jeddito District	Mammal bone		793		93.7
(This paper)	Bird bone		30		3.5
	Mammal/Bird bone		23		2.7
		Total	846	Total	99.9

implement was embellished. This is an awl made from a metatarsal of mule deer. The joint (butt) has been carved to form a dog (?) effigy with inlaid turquoise eyes and an arched tail above an oval perforation and an encircling band of incised crisscross lines which form small squares (fig. 5). It is an attractive as well as intriguing artifact, but I must concede that it is put in the shade by several scrapers inlaid with shell, jet, and turquoise and dazzlingly polished that were recovered from Pueblo Bonito by Judd (1954, pl. 34).

The bone ornaments in the Jeddito assemblage, limited to tubular and flat rectangular beads and to pendants, are reasonably well turned out but rarely decorated. Only one bead in the collection carries a shallowly carved herringbone motif (fig. 18d), and but five beads bear one or more incised lines.

Until recent times, there was a tendency among the smaller, more isolated human societies to emphasize a certain aspect of culture and one or two modes of artistic expression above all other possible ones. In prehistoric and early historic Awatovi and in the neighboring villages, the ceremonial system was all-important: it provided for the abundant rainfall and plentiful crops so vital to these subsistence farming peoples living in a semiarid climate; it also guaranteed that they would be free of disease, and it was the basis of their belief in the continuity of life after death (Titiev 1944, pp. 176-178). The public ceremonies in the annual calendar of ritual songs and "dances," with the many participants of all ages wearing colorful costumes, took place in the village plazas. But the secret parts of the rituals, preceding the public ceremonies, transpired in the clan kivas or ceremonial chambers.

Much attention was paid, at Awatovi and nearby Kawaika-a, to the execution of elaborate polychrome geometric and pictorial designs on many of their freshly plastered kiva walls. Statistical analyses of pottery types distributed in the fills of the painted kivas showed that the earliest group of these kivas, in the upper part of the Western Mound at Awatovi, represented the early phase of Pueblo IV; that the next and later group, at Kawaika-a and in the area between the Western and Eastern mounds at Awatovi, represented the standard or "classic" phase of Pueblo IV and was notable for the emergence of distinctive Sikyatki Polychrome pottery, albeit in a proportion of only 5 to 15 percent; and that the latest group of painted kivas occurred within the pre-Spanish, seventeenth-century section of Awatovi, with Sikyatki Polychrome running in proportions from 5 to 10 percent. The correct chronological placement of the three groups of Jeddito kivas based on pottery typology was borne out by the results of the wholly independent analysis of wall painting styles and was corroborated, insofar as this was possible, by the few available tree-ring dates from several Awatovi kivas (Smith 1952, pp. 316-319).

An older art form was evidenced at the Jeddito sites by the vast quantities of whole and broken corrugated and painted pottery vessels of different shapes and sizes that served both utilitarian and ceremonial purposes. At Awatovi, black-on-white pottery with geometric designs suggesting basketry origins first appeared in the Western Mound at the beginning of the twelfth century A.D., and painted pottery of numerous types continued to show up in unbroken series for six centuries, culminating in Awatovi Black-on-yellow, notable for layouts with markedly bold and ingenious design motifs, until the village was ultimately abandoned in A.D. 1700 (Smith 1971).

With a persistent and vigorous pottery industry and a late-blooming, corruscating kiva mural art to absorb their artistic energy, it is remarkable that the Jeddito peoples were able also to devote so much skill and care to their bone and antler industries — and to their stone industry as well — as the products of these industries amply demonstrate.

CATALOGUE NUMBERS OF
ILLUSTRATED ARTIFACTS

Figure 3:   a. 644 36-131-10/8933
            b. 183 36-131-10/8909
            c. B3306 38-120-10/16110
            d. 2033 36-131-10/9342
            e. 472 37-111-10/12135
            f. 1749 37-111-10/12173
            g. B7874 39-97-10/20205
            h. 968 36-131-10/9095
            i. 174 36-131-10/8912
            j. B9241 39-97-10/20537
            k. 2091 36-131-10/9399
            l. 628 36-131-10/9014
            m. 35-126-10/5566
            n. 1791 37-111-10/12154
            o. 2020 36-131-10/9329
            p. 646 36-131-10/9020
Figure 4:   *Left*, 642 36-131-10/8931
            Right, B7916 39-97-10/19942
Figure 5:   B8622 39-97-10/20419
Figure 6:   *Left*, B7911 39-97-10/19994
            Right, B7931 39-97-10/19957
Figure 7:   a. 2032 36-131-10/9341
            b. 2041 36-131-10/9350
            c. B7884 39-97-10/20194
            d. B7870 39-97-10/20191
Figure 8:   a. 204 36-131-10/8948
            b. B3820 38-120-10/16142
            c. B4187 38-120-10/16194
            d. B8582 39-97-10/20029
Figure 9:   a. 379 36-131-10/8993
            b. 2054 36-131-10/9363
            c. 573 35-126-10/5889
            d. B8475 39-97-10/19971
            e. 631 36-131-10/9017
Figure 10: a. B7972 39-9740/20010
            b. B3886 38-120-10/16187
            c. 1933 36-131-10/9105
Figure 11: *Left*, B8174 39-97-10/20006
            Right, B7334 39-97-10/20033
Figure 12: a. B7347 39-97-10/20339
            b. 1993 36-131-10/8964
            c. B7573 39-97-10/20346
            d. 2138 36-131-10/9430
            e. B4478 38-120-10/16064
            f. B8771 39-97-10/20446
            g. 76 36-131-10/9135
            h. B3466 38-120-10/16136
Figure 13: a. B4337 38-120-10/16256
            b. 915 36-131-10/9111
            c. 859 36-131-10/9116
            d. 917 36-131-10/9205
            e. 990 36-131-10/9114
            f. 1019 36-131-10/8882
            g. B9166 39-97-10/20529
            h. B8523 39-97-10/20026
            i. B7390 39-97-10/20190

Figure 14: a. 565 35-126-10/5881
            b. B4498 38-120-10/16261
            c. 1926 36-131-10/9085
            d. 588 35-126-10/5904
            e. 215 36-131-10/9143
            f. 499 37-111-10/12375
            g. B3173 39-97-10/16376
            h. 611 35-126-10/5930
            i. B8172 39-97-10/20058
Figure 15: a. 689 36-131-10/9193
            b. 176 36-131-10/9192
            c. B3865 38-120-10/16244
            d. 1665 37-111-10/12353
Figure 16: a. B7933 97-97-10/20073
            b. B4191 38-120-10/16259
            c. B3612 38-120-10/16330
            d. 35-126-10/5929
            e. 1812 37-111-10/12317
            f. 861 36-131-10/19213
            g. B3627 38-120-10/16257
Figure 17: a. 1999 36-131-10/9191
            b. B3788 38-120-10/16382
            c. 659 35-126-10/6003
            d. B2561 38-120-10/16326
Figure 18: a. B9196 39-97-10/20293
            b. B3741 38-120-10/16285
            c. B3887 38-120-10/16390
            d. B2087 38-120-10/16331
            e. 1524 37-111-10/12286
            f. 1009 36-131-10/9177
            g. B8025 39-97-10/20054
            h. B7863 39-97-10/19920
            i. 1519 37-111-10/12319
            j. 473c 37-111-10/12308
            k. 473b 37-111-10/12308
            l. 1085 36-131-10/9210
            m. B4154 38-120-10/17854
            n. 1515 37-111-10/12300
            o. B7964 39-97-10/20045
            p. B4166 38-120-10/16398
            q. B9175 39-97-10/20540
Figure 19: a. B3313 38-120-10/16379
            b. 875 36-131-10/9233
            c. 617 35-126-10/5933
            d. 673 36-131-10/9226
            e. 1971 36-131-10/9232
            f. 1793 37-111-10/12345
Figure 20: a. 1535 37-111-10/12443
            b. 908 37-111-10/12392
            c. B7977 39-97-10/19919
            d. 660 37-111-10/12368
            e. B4228 38-120-10/16370
            f. 1228 37-111-10/12373
            g. 932 37-111-10/12357
            h. 681 36-131-10/9141
            i. 1790 37-111-10/12366
            j. 597 37-111-10/12377
            k. 911 37-111-10/12374

References

Brew, J.O.
  1946 *Archaeology of Alkali Ridge, Southeastern Utah.* Papers of the Peabody Museum, Harvard University, vol. 21.

Hayes, A.C., and J.A. Lancaster
  1975 *Badger House Community, Mesa Verde National Park, Colorado.* Publication in Archeology 7E. Wetherill Mesa Studies, National Park Service, Washington, D.C.

Hodge, F.W.
  1920 *Hawikuh Bonework, Indian Notes,* vol. 3. Museum of the American Indian, Heye Foundation, New York.

Judd, N.M.
  1954 *The Material Culture of Pueblo Bonito.* Smithsonian Miscellaneous Collections, vol. 124, Washington, D.C.

  1959 *Pueblo del Arroyo, Chaco Canyon, New Mexico.* Smithsonian Miscellaneous Collections, vol. 138, no. 1, Washington, D.C.

Kidder, A.V.
  1932 *The Artifacts of Pecos.* Yale University Press, New Haven.

Morris, E.H.
  1919 *The Aztec Ruin.* American Museum of Natural History, Anthropological Papers, vol. 26, pt. 1, pp. 1-108, New York.

  1939 *Archaeological Studies in the La Plata District, Southwestern Colorado and Northwestern New Mexico.* Carnegie Institution of Washington, Publication 519, Washington, D.C.

Olsen, S.J.
  1976 The Dogs of Awatovi, *"American Antiquity,"* vol. 41, no. 1, pp. 102-106, Washington, D.C.

Smith, Watson
  1952 *Kiva Mural Decorations at Awatovi and Kawaika-a.* Papers of the Peabody Museum, Harvard University, vol. 37.

  1971 *Painted Ceramics of the Western Mound at Awatovi.* Papers of the Peabody Museum, Harvard University, vol. 38.

Titiev, M.
  1944 *Old Oraibi: A Study of the Hopi Indians of the Third Mesa.* Papers of the Peabody Museum, Harvard University, vol. 22, no. 1.

Woodbury, R.B.
  1954 *Prehistoric Stone Implements of Northeastern Arizona.* Papers of the Peabody Museum, Harvard University, vol. 34.